HIDDEN DIFFERENCES

DOING BUSINESS WITH THE JAPANESE

Books by Edward T. Hall

THE DANCE OF LIFE
BEYOND CULTURE
THE HIDDEN DIMENSION
THE SILENT LANGUAGE

With Mildred Reed Hall

THE FOURTH DIMENSION IN ARCHITECTURE:
The Impact of Building on Man's Behavior

HIDDEN DIFFERENCES

DOING BUSINESS WITH THE JAPANESE

吉

**EDWARD T. HALL and
MILDRED REED HALL**

ANCHOR BOOKS

A DIVISION OF RANDOM HOUSE, INC.

NEW YORK

ANCHOR BOOKS EDITIONS, 1987, 1990

Copyright © 1987 by Edward T. Hall and Mildred Reed Hall

All rights reserved under International and Pan-American Copyright
Conventions. Published in the United States by Anchor Books, a
division of Random House, Inc., New York, and simultaneously in
Canada by Random House of Canada Limited, Toronto. Originally
published in hardcover in the United States by Anchor Books in 1987.

Anchor Books and colophon are registered trademarks of Random House, Inc.

Some portions of the material in this book appeared in different form in the
following books:
Verborgene Signale: Über den Umgang mit Japanern, by EDWARD T.
HALL and MILDRED REED HALL
    Copyright © 1985 by Edward T. Hall Associates
    Published by Stern/Gruner & Jahr

The Dance of Life, by EDWARD T. HALL
    Copyright © 1983 by Edward T. Hall Associates
    Published by Anchor Books/Doubleday

Beyond Culture, by EDWARD T. HALL
    Copyright © 1976 by Edward T. Hall
    Published by Anchor Books/Doubleday

Library of Congress Cataloging-in-Publication Data
Hall, Edward Twitchell.
  Hidden differences.
  Includes index.
  1. Communication—Japan—International communication.
2. National characteristics, Japanese. 3. Intercultural
communication. 4. Businessmen—United States—Attitudes.
5. Businessmen—Japan—Attitudes. 6. Japan—Relations—
United States. 7. United States—Relations—Japan.
I. Hall, Mildred Reed. II. Title. III. Title:
Understanding the Japanese and how to do business with
them.
P96.152J335 1987   001.51′0952   86-20610
ISBN 0-385-23884-3

www.anchorbooks.com

Printed in the United States of America
20 19 18 17 16 15 14 13 12 11

CONTENTS

Part II THE JAPANESE

Part III JAPANESE BUSINESS

Part IV THE AMERICAN COMPANY IN JAPAN

PREFACE

友 This is a book for American business executives interacting with Japanese—a book that clarifies the often baffling Japanese culture. Too often, business relationships suffer because Americans fail to understand Japanese psychology and behavior, an understandable failing given the many hidden differences between the two cultures. We hope to clarify those differences for professionals by describing and analyzing behavior and critical incidents in the real world of business, rather than by probing the culture's economics, politics, or sociology.

This book can be helpful to any businessperson who is contemplating involvement with the Japanese market. It should be especially useful to top management. They are the people ultimately responsible for their companies' overall performances and economic health, as well as for their future success. Management's insights and sensitivity are crucial during the early, critical phases of operations in Japan; a gram of insight at the top is worth a kilo at the lower levels. Management can establish the approach; if they pay attention to the message of this book, the rest of the company will follow suit. To that end, we have written a book expressing ideas, many of which a conscientious chief executive officer knows or would like to communicate to subordinates but may have difficulty expressing in words.

International expansion poses complex problems—problems that are worth tackling. As one experienced vice-president, the head of international operations for a large firm, commented, "Foreign operations are my most difficult assignment, day in and day out, and may even hold greater long-range potential for sales and profit than the domestic business."

For the past thirty years the authors have worked as a team in the field of intercultural communication, designing programs for the selection and training of individuals working in foreign cultures, consulting to international business, and writing books and articles on the intercultural process. We specialize in identifying the nonverbal components of intercultural communication—the unspoken signals and assumptions that flow from people's psychology and national character—that are crucial to success in business.

This book grew out of a series of books we wrote for the German publisher Gruner & Jahr on the psychology, communication styles, and hidden traps that are encountered at the cultural interface between German businesspeople and their American, French, and Japanese counterparts. The series, *"Verborgene Signale"* ("Hidden Differences"), consisted of three sets of books for German business which Gruner & Jahr published in German-language editions: *How to Communicate with the Americans, How to Communicate with the French,* and *How to Communicate with the Japanese.* Each of these had a companion volume on how to communicate with the Germans: for Americans (in English), for the French (in French), and for the Japanese (in Japanese). After the last of the series appeared in March 1985, the prestigious Japanese publishing house Bungei Shunju asked us to prepare two volumes on communication between the Japanese and the Americans, to be published in Japanese and English.

A half century of study and research at the intercultural interface by Edward T. Hall reveals that one of the most basic of all cultural differences concerns information: what it is, what forms it takes, how it is handled. Information is not just one thing or even one category of events. It is both a product of culture and drastically altered by that culture. For example, Hispanics in New Mexico represent a kind of culture in which all information is widely shared. The members of this group have a great psychological need to be in the know, to stay informed about everything and everyone; they share this trait with other cultures such as the Japanese. Northern Europeans and Americans, on the other hand, compartmentalize and seal information away from other people. As a result, the information flow is restricted. This difference is far from trivial; indeed, it pervades all of society, and ignorance of the difference has caused many a blunder, as we shall see.

This book is divided into four parts:

Part I, "Key Concepts," serves as the code breaker for the description of the culture that follows. The reader should resist the temptation to skip this section and to plunge immediately into what appears to be the meat of the book. The life patterns of a complex civilization cannot be covered in two hundred pages. Nevertheless, it is possible to describe a number of the principal contrasting patterns and to give examples that can serve as conceptual frames. When viewed through the frames of Part I, the specific examples in Parts II to IV become far more useful; they can be seen as representatives of larger patterns instead of isolated fragments or mere generalizations. Part I is designed to bring into focus selected elements of thought and behavior—especially those patterns that are at variance with American culture and that have proved to be stumbling blocks on the road to understanding.

Part II, "The Japanese," describes some of the major contrasts between American and Japanese behavior within the broader context of cultural differences as set forth in Part I.

Part III, "Japanese Business," describes both the relation of Japanese business to its government and the organization of individual companies. It tells how business decisions are

made and describes the crucial relationship between the
worker and the company.

Part IV, "The American Company in Japan," tells what an
American business should know to succeed in the Japanese
market.

ACKNOWLEDGMENTS

As part of our research for this book, we conducted interviews in the United States and in Japan. We were most fortunate to have the cooperation of a wide range of exceptionally talented and knowledgeable executives, men and women with years of hands-on experience in business. We wish to acknowledge their assistance and to express our thanks. Their insights and experience helped shape this book, and we are indeed grateful for their cooperation and their honesty.

In Tokyo, we had the advice and assistance of the late Dr. Hiroshi Wagatsuma, a distinguished colleague and dear friend, who was Professor of Cultural Anthropology, Center for Humanities and Social Sciences, Tokyo Institute of Technology. Without Prof. Wagatsuma's advice, assistance, and support this project would not have been possible.

Another colleague to whom we are indebted for assistance is the well-known linguist Professor Eleanor Jorden of Cornell University. She reviewed our manuscript, and her cogent comments and suggestions strengthened the book. We acknowledge her contributions with thanks. However, we take full responsibility for any errors or omissions.

We are especially grateful for the fine spirit of cooperation, support, and encouragement for this project that we found in Mr. Shuji Takeuchi, Editor in Chief of Bungei Shunju.

It was our great fortune to have two excellent interpreters, Junko Yagasaki and Hiroshi Yoneyama, who did an outstanding job. These young people brought intelligence and insight

to their work and assisted us in many ways beyond their
duties as translators and interpreters. Both are now Fulbright
doctoral candidates studying in the United States.

We wish to thank Judy Karasik for editing the manuscript
and for her many valuable suggestions. We also thank our
assistant, Jana Oyler, for her diligence in research, for running
our office during our many trips, and for her skills in preparing
the manuscript for publication.

Sally Arteseros, Senior Editor at Doubleday & Company,
was especially helpful in the publication of this book in the
United States. Once again we thank her for her loyal support
and encouragement.

EDWARD T. HALL and MILDRED REED HALL

INTRODUCTION

友 This book is an introduction to Japanese culture, custom-crafted for the American reader. It is specific exclusively to Japan and may be applied nowhere else. Our observations are based on the distilled knowledge and experience of men and women with years of successful overseas business experience, people who have succeeded where others have failed. Their practical experience has been augmented and reinforced by our own knowledge and experience. Don't be surprised if some of the ideas seem strange to you or possibly even insignificant at first. If they do, be wary, for many of these concepts which may at first seem unimportant to Americans are frequently the things to which they should pay the closest attention.

CASE HISTORY: An American company with a Japanese subsidiary chose one of its best young men to head the Tokyo office. His predecessor had been an older Japanese who had been with the company many years until illness forced his retirement. The new man, whom we will call Thompson, arrived determined to "bring the Tokyo office up to speed." Thompson was in his late thirties and flush with success from his performance in the New York office. On the flight to Japan he made plans for reorganizing the Tokyo operation and arrived eager to take charge.

Thompson's first important decision concerned the spring advertising campaign. When he met with the Japanese agency handling his company's account, their proposal was totally unacceptable to him; their ads seemed to have nothing to do with the product. Thompson was bewildered. "How could anyone know what our product is from these ads?" he asked. Thompson sent a telex to New York critical of the campaign. He felt angry and frustrated when New York telephoned advising him to follow the agency's advice.

Within a few weeks Thompson discovered what he termed "serious management problems." Nothing seemed to be going well and staff morale was poor. The office was becoming chaotic. Meetings were disorganized, nobody followed an agenda, and department heads seemed not to know their plans for the next quarter. His requests for information were met with vague promises—"We will do our best"—but no hard data were forthcoming. All his efforts to reorganize the office were resisted.

Six months later, his top Japanese manager resigned. This action brought things to a complete halt. Sales kept dropping and there were problems with distributors. Thompson was recalled. Eventually, with the help of a Tokyo management consulting firm, the company hired a Japanese to replace Thompson.

◄◄►►

An analysis of the above situation reveals many errors. The first mistake made was the company's in its decision to send a young man to head their Tokyo office. The Japanese respect age and experience and don't consider someone in his thirties qualified for such an important job. The second mistake was in not insisting that Thompson prepare himself with extensive background reading and courses in Japanese language and culture. The third mistake was in sending a "hard hitter" who wanted to put his stamp on the Tokyo office; the Japa-

nese find aggressive, ambitious young people uncongenial
and disruptive.

Thompson himself failed on many counts. His greatest
error was that he didn't seek the advice and help of his top
Japanese manager, nor did he avail himself of information
from JETRO, the American Chamber of Commerce, or the
American Embassy, all rich sources of aid. The fact that doing
business in Japan is a whole new ball game never seemed to
cross his mind. In not respecting organizational hierarchy in
the office, he made a grave tactical error which he never
recognized but which alienated everyone. When his top Japanese manager quit, he should have seen that he was in deep
trouble. Yet another mistake was his choosing to learn nothing about Japanese advertising. He did nothing to avail himself of the large amount of useful information about Japanese
business in any of the many books that are well known and
widely available. It is doubtful that he even understood his
part in the slowing of business during his months in Tokyo.

Despite popular beliefs to the contrary, the single greatest
barrier to business success is the one erected by culture. Each
culture has a hidden code of behavior that can rarely be
understood without a code breaker. Even though every culture is experienced personally—indeed, few individuals see
its commonality—it is nonetheless a shared system. Members
of a common culture not only share information, they share
methods of coding, storing, and retrieving that information.
Some 80 to 90 percent of the significant features of a culture
are reflected in its nonverbal messages. These are usually
taken for granted and transmitted unconsciously. Nonverbal
messages are highly situational in character. Furthermore, the
meanings of such messages are unique to each culture and
often are charged with emotion.

Business depends for its life on information, so anything
interfering with the communication process, the way in
which people transmit or withhold and control information,

can ultimately cripple any transaction. The transmission of business information between different cultures is threatened by different behavioral signals as well as by different languages. This is true in all international business and is further complicated in Japan by the fact that Japanese business can never be evaluated simply in terms of the bottom line. First and foremost, it depends on what transpires between people, on personal interactions within power and influence networks.

In the past two years we have conducted 165 in-depth, open-ended interviews with a carefully selected sample of individuals from business and the professions in the United States and Japan. Making detailed observations of how people behave and relate to each other in a wide range of situations, we assembled the raw data on which our later analysis is based. The reader may wonder how we can make detailed observations based largely on interviews. Actually, to the researcher the interview is like two sides of a coin. First, there is the verbal behavior, the content of the interview itself; then there is everything else that goes on: the setting, the timing, the decor, body language, what had to be done in order to set up the interview. In fact, the whole nonverbal component contains at least as much information as—and sometimes more than—the interview itself.

One of the purposes of this book is to increase general awareness of the whole nonverbal side of the communication process. With the help of local experts in the analysis of our data, our samples are also reinforced by interviews with writers, artists, and educators. This combination of interviews, observation, and analysis, backed by years of experience in the intercultural field, makes it possible to identify a significant proportion of the major cultural patterns that American business executives should be aware of when dealing with the Japanese.

One must begin with the fact that cultures are unified

wholes in which everything interrelates. Experience has taught us that in the search for patterns it is vital to overlook nothing and to take nothing for granted. We work with data from a broad range of information sources: for example, how business is conducted, how hotels and transit systems are run, what newspapers, magazines, film, and television tell us. The reader may ask what we are looking for in our interviews. The answer is, we're looking for patterns, and in order to find patterns, one needs a lot of data. To illustrate: once when we were discussing Arab cultural patterns with a well-known Middle East specialist and former ambassador, the ambassador observed: "It's pretty much like watching a merry-go-round. At first you think that the white horse follows the gray horse. When you've seen it go around several times, it becomes evident that the gray horse really follows the white horse." That is a pattern. We pay particular attention to how information flows, either freely or through restricted channels; whether power is centralized or diffused; how decisions are made and by whom; how people conduct interpersonal relationships; how much close personal contact and confidence exist between people.

At this point the matter of what we mean by "Japanese" and what is meant by "American" should be dealt with. Even when one is referring to a particular group of Americans it is much harder to define the Americans than the more homogeneous Japanese. Because of the many individual, regional, ethnic, and cultural differences in a large country like the United States, the term "American" has a very broad connotation. While there are always exceptions, in this book when we refer to Americans we are talking about those involved in the most representative group of American business working overseas—Americans of northern European heritage. When we refer to the Japanese we are talking about the Japanese businessmen working in large metropolitan areas such as

Tokyo and Yokohama, and in New York, Los Angeles, and San Francisco.

There are many books on Japan, and more being published every month. Unfortunately, few of them agree and seldom do they give the same picture. We have sifted through the morass of conflicting statements with great care and selected those books which most closely approach the needs of our readers. It should also be understood that the fact that there are so many different interpretations of Japanese culture simply reflects the varied situational biases of the writers, to say nothing of their varying degrees of expertise in Japanese culture.

We have no particular theoretical, ideological, or political bias. Our objective is to make a contribution to international understanding and to help reduce the tensions that result from the many different "silent languages" that people use. Our goal is to maximize success for American business executives in Japan and to identify some of the hidden obstacles on which numerous companies have already foundered.

Part I 吉

KEY CONCEPTS

CULTURE IS COMMUNICATION

友 In physics today, so far as we know, the galaxies that one studies are all controlled by the same laws. This is not true of the worlds created by mankind. Each cultural world operates according to its own internal dynamic, its own principles, and its own laws—written and unwritten. Even the dimensions of time and space are unique to each culture. There are, however, some common threads that run through all cultures.

Any culture is primarily a system for creating, sending, storing, and processing information. Communication underlies everything. Although we tend to regard language as the main channel of communication, research reveals that anywhere from 80 to 90 percent of information is communicated by other means.

The world of communication is divided into three parts: words, material things, and behavior. Words are the medium of business, politics, and diplomacy. Material things are usually indicators of status and power. Behavior provides feedback on how others feel and includes techniques for avoiding confrontation.

By studying these things in our own and other cultures, we can come to understand a vast, unexplored region of human behavior that exists outside the range of people's conscious awareness: informatics. This field includes a broad range of evolutionary and emergent ideas, practices, and solutions to problems which have their roots not in the lofty ideas of

philosophers but in the common clay of the shared experiences of ordinary people. They are practical as well as fasci-
nating; the study of Japanese informatics will greatly benefit
American business.

If we do not pay attention to these elements, not only will
we learn nothing of informatics, but the system of culture will
not work for us, whether we are in our native culture or
another. Culture can be likened to an enormous, subtle, extraordinarily complex computer. It programs the actions and
responses of every person, and these programs must be mastered by anyone wishing to make the system work.

"Making the system work" requires attention to everything
people do to survive, advance in the world, and gain satisfaction from life. Failure can often be attributed to one of the
following errors:

1. Leaving out crucial steps because one hasn't truly mastered the system
2. Unconsciously applying one's own rules to another system, which never works
3. Deliberately rejecting the rules—written or unwritten—
   and trying to force one's own rules on another system
4. Changes and/or breakdowns of the system in times of
   political upheaval, economic collapse, war, and revolution

Cultural communications are deeper and more complex
than spoken or written messages. The essence of cross-cultural communication has more to do with releasing responses
than with sending messages. *It is more important to release
the right response than to send the "right message."* We
offer here some conceptual tools to help Americans decipher
the complex and unspoken messages of the Japanese culture.

FAST AND SLOW MESSAGES:
FINDING THE APPROPRIATE SPEED

友   Since information underlies virtually everything, it is not surprising that the speed with which a particular message can be decoded and acted on is an important factor in human communication. Therefore, one would expect to find that there are fast and slow messages—which is precisely the case. A headline or cartoon, for example, is fast. On the other hand, the meaning that one extracts from books or art is slow. A fast message sent to people who are geared to a slow format will usually miss the target. While the content of the wrong-speed message may be understandable, it won't be received by someone tuned to a different frequency. The problem is that few people are even aware that such frequencies exist.

EXAMPLES OF FAST AND SLOW MESSAGES

Fast Messages	Slow Messages
Prose	Poetry
Headlines	Books
A communiqué	An ambassador
Propaganda	Art
Cartoons	Etchings
TV commercials	TV documentary

Fast Messages	*Slow Messages*
Television	Print
Quick, easy familiarity	Slow, deep relationships
Ideologies	Culture

Almost everything in life can be placed somewhere along the fast/slow message-speed spectrum. Such things as diplomacy, research, writing books, and creating art are accomplished in the slow mode. Buddha, Confucius, Shakespeare, Goethe, and Rembrandt all produced messages that we are still in the process of deciphering hundreds of years after the fact. Bear in mind also that the underlying message of any language system can only be perceived very slowly. After four thousand years, human beings are just beginning to discover what language is all about. The same can be said of culture, which incorporates multiple styles of "languages" that only release messages very, very slowly. Some cultures are understood more slowly than others. It can take years before an American can assemble enough data and enough understanding to "read" the Japanese at even the elementary level. In fact, there are some Americans who unfortunately never do "get the message." This is in part because for Americans Japan is a slow message.

A person is in essence also a slow message; it takes some time to get to know someone well. This is, of course, truer in some cultures than in others. In Japan, personal relationships and friendships tend to take a long time to solidify. This is largely a function of the hierarchical system in Japan, which integrates many Japanese into close-knit networks of schoolmates and relatives. It is extraordinarily difficult, if not impossible, for a foreigner to break into these networks. Nevertheless, the businessman from America would do well to attempt to be close friends with the Japanese, for whom closeness in relationships is a well-developed drive.

In countries such as the United States, developing friendships is easy enough. In fact, people in this country can become friends in a very short period of time. However, a study on the subject, conducted by Edward T. Hall for the U.S. State Department, revealed that a worldwide complaint about Americans was that they seemed capable of forming only one kind of friendship: the informal, superficial kind that does not involve an exchange of deep confidences. Of course, there are exceptions, but as a rule Americans are very different from their Japanese counterparts in this regard. In this sense, then, Americans will have to take longer to "read" the Japanese than they are accustomed to.

HIGH AND LOW CONTEXTS:
HOW MUCH INFORMATION IS
ENOUGH?

友 "Context" is the information that surrounds an event and is inextricably bound up with the meaning of that event. The elements that combine to produce a given meaning—events and context—are in different proportions depending on the culture. It is thus possible to order the cultures of the world on a scale from high to low context.

"A high context (HC) communication or message is one in which *most* of the information is already in the person, while very little is in the coded, explicit, transmitted part of the message. A low context (LC) communication is just the opposite; i.e., the mass of the information is vested in the explicit code. Twins who have grown up together can and do communicate more economically (HC) than two lawyers in a courtroom during a trial (LC), a mathematician programming a computer, two politicians drafting legislation, two administrators writing a regulation."

Edward T. Hall, 1976

◄◄►►

Japanese, Arab, and Mediterranean peoples who have extensive information networks among family, friends, colleagues, and clients, and who are involved in close personal relationships, are "high-context" (HC). As a result, for most normal transactions in daily life they do not require, nor do they expect, much in-depth background information. This is because it is their nature to keep themselves informed about everything having to do with the people who are important in their lives. Low-context people include the Americans and the Germans, Swiss, Scandinavians, and other northern Europeans. Within each culture, of course, there are specific individual differences in the need for contexting—that is, the process of filling in background data—but it is helpful to know whether or not the culture of a particular country falls on the high or low side of the scale.

Contexting performs multiple functions beyond those already described. For example, any shift in the level of context is a communication. The shift can be up the scale, indicating a warming of the relationship, or down the scale (lowering the context), communicating coolness or displeasure—signaling that something has gone wrong with a relationship. For example, the boss who is annoyed with his assistant and shifts from the high-context, familiar form of address to the low-context, formal form of address is telling the assistant in no uncertain terms that he has stepped out of line and incurred disfavor in the boss's eyes. Moving in the high-context direction is a source of daily feedback in Japan as to how things are going. The day starts with the use of honorifics (formal forms of address attached to the name). If things are going well the honorifics are dropped as the day progresses. First-naming in the United States is an artificial attempt at high-contexting which is not really appreciated by the Japanese (or most other foreign peoples). One is always safe using a formal form of address in Japan. Insofar as we have been able to test our assumptions concerning the significance of high and low contexting, the rules are universal.

Many white Americans are low-context. American culture does not favor extensive, well-developed, informal information networks. We do have them, but in comparison with the Japanese ours are limited in scope and development. What follows from this is that Americans feel the need to be contexted any time they are asked to do something or to make a decision. This need for detailed background information stems from the fact that the American approach to life is quite segmented and focuses on discrete, compartmentalized bits of information. Americans need to know what is going to be in that compartment before they commit themselves. The authors experienced this need in Japan when we were asked to supply names of Japanese and Americans for a small conference. Like most prudent Americans, we were reluctant to provide names until we knew what the conference was about and what the individuals recommended would be expected to do. This seemed logical and reasonable enough to us. Nevertheless, our reluctance was interpreted as being diffi-

cult and possibly even obstructionist by our Japanese colleagues. To their way of thinking the mere presence of certain
individuals endows the group and its activities with authority
and status, while Americans tend to place more importance
on the agenda and on the relevance of the expertise of different individuals to that agenda.

Another example of the contrast between how HC and LC
systems work is this: consider a top American executive
working in an office and receiving his normal quota of visitors, usually one at a time. Most of the information that is
relevant to his job originates from the few people he sees in
the course of the day, as well as from what he reads. This is
why the advisors who surround American company presidents are so important, for they, and they alone, control the
content and the flow of information to the chief executive.

Contrast this with the office of a Japanese businessman,
where even vice-presidents and other top managers share
offices so they can share information. Not only are other
people constantly coming and going, both seeking and giving
information, but the entire form and function of the organization is centered on gathering, processing, and disseminating
information. Everyone stays informed about every aspect of
the business and knows who is best informed on what subjects.

To give another example, in Germany virtually everything
is low-context and compartmentalized. The executive office
is both a refuge and a screen—a refuge for the boss from the
distractions of day-to-day office interactions, and a screen for
the employees from continual supervision. Information communicated in the office is not shared except with a select few
—the exact antithesis of the Japanese high-context approach
that places them in a sea of information. The Germans, and to
a lesser extent the Americans, produce and work with islands
of information.

HC people are apt to become impatient and irritated when

LC people insist on giving them information they don't need. Conversely, low-context people are at a loss when high-context people do not provide *enough* information. One of the great communications challenges in life is to find the appropriate level of contexting which is customary both at home and abroad. Too much information frequently leads people to feel they are being talked down to; too little information can mystify them or make them feel left out. Ordinarily, people make these adjustments automatically in their own country, but in other countries their messages frequently miss the target.

The other side of the coin, when considering context level, is the apparent paradox that high-context people like the Japanese, when considering or evaluating a new enterprise, want to see *everything*. Annual reports or even tax returns are not enough. Furthermore, they will keep asking until they get the information they want. Being high-context, the Japanese need to make their own synthesis of the meanings of the figures. Unlike the Americans, they feel uncomfortable with someone else's synthesis, someone else's "bottom line."

SPACE

友 Every living thing has a visible physical boundary—its skin—separating it from its external environment. This visible boundary is surrounded by a series of invisible boundaries that are more difficult to define but are just as real. These other boundaries begin with the individual's personal space and terminate with his individual "territory."

TERRITORIALITY

Territoriality in animals is the act of laying claim to and defending a territory. It is a vital link in the chain of events necessary for survival. In humans territoriality is highly developed and strongly influenced by culture. It is strong in all humans, but is particularly strong in American culture. In the traditional American family a woman's feelings about her kitchen and her home, and a man's feelings about his particular chair, his office and desk, or his study are strictly territorial.

Space also communicates power. A corner office suite in the United States is conventionally occupied by "the brass." A private office has more status than a desk in the open without walls. The top floors are reserved for high-ranking officials and executives. In Japan, however, top Japanese executives rarely use their private offices except for meetings with outsiders. They prefer to work in large open areas, surrounded by colleagues, to insure constant interaction and information flow. Being a group-oriented people, the Japanese have made their spaces reflect a community bias. Private offices are not the norm in Japan.

PERSONAL SPACE

Personal space is another form of territory. Each person has around him an invisible bubble of space which expands and contracts depending on his relationship to those around him, his emotional state, his cultural background, and the activity he is performing. Few people are allowed to penetrate this bit of mobile territory, and then only for short periods of time. Changes in the bubble brought about by cramped quarters or crowding cause people to feel uncomfortable or aggressive. In northern Europe, the bubbles are quite large; moving south to France, Italy, Greece, and Spain, the bubbles get smaller and smaller so that the distance that is perceived as intimate in the north overlaps personal distance in the south, which means that Mediterranean Europeans "get too close" to the Germans, the Scandinavians, the English, and Americans of northern European ancestry. Moving around the world to Japan, everything changes. The personal bubble is transmuted into an organizational bubble, so that three vice-presidents working in a single small office can share everything. The Japanese do have a personal space; however, the actual distance is not as important as other signs of rank and intimacy such as the depth of a bow or the language being used. The Japanese accept high density and a degree of crowding in public spaces that would be unacceptable to Americans. Their houses, apartments, and offices are usually smaller and more crowded than our own. Their subways and trains are often packed with people. Cultural differences in the size and penetrability of the space bubble are some of the great unconscious irritants that must be overcome when working in Japan.

THE MULTISENSORY SPATIAL EXPERIENCE

Few people realize that space is perceived by *all* the senses, not by vision alone. Auditory space is perceived by the ears, thermal space by the skin, kinesthetic space by the muscles, and olfactory space by the nose. Americans to some extent and Germans to a greater extent rely heavily on auditory screening, particularly when they want to concentrate. Again, as one might imagine, there are great cultural differences in the programming of the senses. High-context peoples, for example, reject auditory screening and thrive on being open to interruptions and in tune with what goes on around them. Hence, in Japanese cities such as Tokyo, one is periodically and "intrusively" bombarded by loudspeakers broadcasting political statements that are experienced by the Americans as "much too loud!" These interruptions—and that is what they are to Americans—cause complaints: "Why do they allow that? Can't somebody do something?"

UNCONSCIOUS REACTIONS
TO SPATIAL DIFFERENCES

All human beings learn literally hundreds of spatial cues as they mature. The meaning of these spatial cues is learned in the context of their own culture. These cues and their associated behaviors are designed to release unconscious responses just as a fragrance might trigger a memory. When people travel and experience how space is handled in other parts of the world, the startling variations they encounter release a visceral response. Since most people don't think about space as being culturally patterned, foreign spatial cues are often misinterpreted and can lead to bad feelings. In fact, these feelings are often displaced onto the people of the country. Feelings Americans have about the way the Japanese handle space will be projected onto the Japanese people in a most personal way. Sometimes when a foreigner appears aggressive or pushy, or remote and cold, it may mean only that his personal distances are different from yours.

Spatial changes give tone to communication, accent it, and at times even override the spoken word. As people interact, the flow and shift of distance between them is integral to the communication process. The normal conversational distance between strangers illustrates the importance of the space dynamics. If a stranger gets "too close," our reaction is automatic—we feel offended or threatened and we back up.

Americans have strong feelings about proximity and the rights, responsibilities, and obligations associated with being a neighbor. One must be "friendly" and neighborly, which means being agreeable, cutting one's lawn, keeping the place up, and doing one's bit for the neighborhood. In Japan, simply sharing adjacent houses does not necessarily mean that people will interact with each other. There's not the kind of visiting back and forth among adults that is common in America. One of the consistent complaints about Japanese businessmen who live in American suburbia is their failure to fulfill neighborly obligations such as keeping their grass cut. Americans see this as an example of the Japanese lack of "public spirit."

TIME

 Life on earth evolved in response to the cycles of day and night and the ebb and flow of the tides. As humans evolved, a multiplicity of internal biological clocks also developed. These biological clocks now regulate most of the physiological functions of our bodies. It is not surprising, therefore, that human concepts of time grew out of the natural rhythms associated with daily, monthly, and annual cycles. In man's early history he was dependent on weather and seasonal changes. From the beginning humans have been tied to growing seasons and were dependent on the forces and rhythms of nature.

Out of this background two time systems evolved—one as an expression of our biological clocks, the other of our environmental cycles. These will be described under the headings "Time as Structure" and "Time as Communication." The former symbolizes our biological clocks in various ways. The latter, which is explicit in all societies and cultures, is based on natural rhythms—the solar, lunar, and annual cycles.

In the sections that follow we restrict ourselves to those manifestations of time that have proved to be stumbling blocks at the cultural interface.

TIME AS STRUCTURE

Monochronic and Polychronic Time

There are many kinds of time systems in the world, but two are most important to international business. We call them monochronic and polychronic time. Monochronic time (M-time) means paying attention to and doing only one thing at a time. Polychronic time (P-time) means being involved with many things at once. Like oil and water, the two systems do not mix.

In monochronic cultures, time is experienced and used in a linear way—comparable to a road extending from the past into the future. M-time is divided quite naturally into segments; it is scheduled and compartmentalized, making it possible for a person to concentrate on one thing at a time. In a monochronic system, the schedule may take on priority above all else and be treated as sacred and unalterable.

M-time is experienced as being almost *tangible:* People talk about it as though it were money, as something that can be "spent," "saved," "wasted," and "lost." It is also used as a classification system for ordering life and setting priorities: "I don't have time to see him." M-time people don't like to be interrupted. Because M-time concentrates on one thing at a time, it can seal people off from one another and, as a result, intensify some relationships while shortchanging others. It is treated as a room which some people are allowed to enter, but from which others are excluded.

M-time dominates most business in the United States. While we perceive M-time as almost in the air we breathe, it is nevertheless a learned product of northern European culture and is therefore arbitrary and imposed. In spite of the fact that it is *learned,* M-time may appear to be natural and logical. The "natural" feelings about M-time stem from the fact that virtually all of us grew up in M-time systems, with whistles and bells counting off the hours. It grew out of the industrial revolution in England and was an artifact of the factory, which required the labor force to be on hand and in place at the appointed hour.

Western cultures, the United States, Switzerland, Germany, and Scandinavia in particular, are dominated by the iron hand of M-time. Germany and Switzerland represent classic examples of M-time cultures, where the percentage of individuals whose personalities fit this pattern seems to be higher than among other peoples of the world. Its manifestations are also apparent in every aspect of American business and social life. Still, M-time is not natural time; in fact, M-time seems to even violate many of man's innate rhythms.

In almost every respect, polychronic (P-time) systems are the antithesis of M-time systems. P-time is characterized by the simultaneous occurrence of many things and by a *great involvement with people.* There is also more emphasis on completing human transactions than on holding to schedules. For example, two polychronic Latins conversing on a street corner would likely opt to be late for their next appointments rather than abruptly terminate the conversation before it came to a natural conclusion. P-time is experienced as much less tangible than M-time, and can better be compared to a single point than to a road.

The Japanese time system combines both M-time and P-time. In their dealings with foreigners and their use of technology, they are quite monochronic; in every other way, especially in interpersonal relations, they are polychronic.

Proper understanding of the difference between the monochronic and polychronic time systems will be helpful in dealing with the time-flexible Japanese. While the generalizations listed below do not apply equally to all cultures, they will help convey a pattern.

Monochronic people	*Polychronic people*
do one thing at a time	do many things at once
concentrate on the job	are highly distractable and subject to interruptions
take time commitments (deadlines, schedules) seriously	consider time commitments an objective to be achieved, if possible
are low-context and need information	are high-context and already have information
are committed to the job	are committed to people and human relationships
adhere religiously to plans	change plans often and easily
are concerned about not disturbing others; follow rules of privacy and consideration	are more concerned with those who are closely related (family, friends, close business associates) than with privacy
show great respect for private property; seldom borrow or lend	borrow and lend things often and easily

| emphasize promptness | base promptness on the relationship |
| are accustomed to short-term relationships | have strong tendency to build lifetime relationships |

The Relation Between Time and Space

In M-time cultures the emphasis is on the compartmental-ization of functions and people. Private offices are sound-proof if possible. In P-time Mediterranean cultures, business offices often have large reception areas where people can wait. Company or government officials may even transact their business by moving about in the reception area, stop-ping to confer with this group and that one until everything has been attended to. In polychronic Japan, private space is to be avoided at all costs because it shuts people off from one another and disrupts the flow of information. In P-time sys-tems, appointments mean very little and may be shifted around even at the last minute to accommodate someone more important in an individual's hierarchy of family, friends, or associates. Some polychronic people (such as Latin Ameri-cans or Arabs) give precedence to their large circle of family members over any business obligation (this is not true of Japanese, who put business first). Polychronic people also have many close friends and good clients with whom they spend a great deal of time. Therefore, if one is in business, it is important to be closely linked to clients or customers. There is a reciprocal feeling of obligation and a need on their part to be helpful. Is it any wonder that P-time people attach so little importance to such things as schedules or agendas? There are other factors, of course, such as the fact that in Japan one of the principal reasons to get together around a table with good food and in congenial surroundings is to strengthen the bonds of friendship and to get to know people.

Polychronic Time and Information

Polychronic people live in a sea of information. They feel they must know the latest about everything and everybody, be it business or personal. Therefore, they tend to be inquisitive.

It is impossible to know how many millions of dollars have been lost in international business because monochronic and polychronic people do not understand each other or even realize that two such time systems exist. The following two examples may illustrate how difficult it is for these two types to relate. While the examples in this case do not derive from Japanese situations, the patterns and principles are applicable.

◄ ◇ ►

A French salesman working for a French company recently bought by Americans found himself with a new American manager who expected instant results. Because of the emphasis on personal relationships, it frequently takes years to develop customers in polychronic France and, in family-owned firms, relationships with customers may span generations. The American manager, not understanding this, ordered the salesman to develop new customers within three months. The salesman knew this was impossible and had to resign, asserting his legal right to take with him all the loyal customers he had developed over the years. Neither side understood what had happened.

◄ ◇ ►

In Mexico, a large American firm had a Mexican manager who, like his countrymen, was polychronic. The top managers traveled from the United States to Mexico City to discuss next year's plans. During the meeting, the agenda, pre-set in the United States, was followed scrupulously. This meant that the Mexican manager was not given an opportunity to resolve questions on which his whole operation depended. His close ties to government and business were vital to the company's future. But his efforts to communicate with American management were thwarted because the Americans had followed the customary practice of sending information out from headquarters, rather than consulting or seeking any advice on the local level. Some of this, of course, was simply bad management, but something else was involved, too. When we came in as consultants to help solve the problem, we found the source of the trouble was a "missing agenda." The Mexican manager was carefully coached on the basics of creating agendas (and getting them recognized beforehand). From then on he was able to participate fully in meetings, giving headquarters all the necessary information.

◄ ◄► ►

Similar differences exist between the United States and Japan. In Japanese meetings the information flow is high, and everyone is expected to read other people's thoughts, to know the state of their business and even what government regulations are in the offing. A tight, fixed agenda can be an encumbrance, even an insult to one's intelligence. Most, if not all, of those present have a pretty good idea of what will be discussed beforehand. The purpose of the meeting is to create consensus. Adherence to a rigid agenda and the achievement of consensus represent opposite goals and do not mix. *The importance of this basic dichotomy cannot be overemphasized.*

Time as a Measure of Competence

In Japan, time on the job is a measure of loyalty to the organization. In America, time on the job can be a measuring rod for competence, effort, and achievement. How long a person holds a job before being promoted is one example; how long he remains in a position of authority and prestige is another. Here is an example of how culture can affect perception: A person of no great intelligence or ambition in the United States can be in a job for years, contributing only the bare minimum; yet the fact that he has been on the job a long time automatically gives him status.

Past- and Future-oriented Countries

It is always important to know which segments of the time frame are emphasized. Cultures in countries such as Iran, India, and those of the Far East are past-oriented. Others, such as that of the urban United States, are oriented to the present and short-term future; and still others, such as those of Latin America, are both past- and present-oriented. In countries such as Germany, where historical background is very important, every talk, book, or article begins with background information giving a historical perspective. This irritates many foreigners, who keep wondering: "Why don't they get on with it? After all, I am educated. Don't the Germans know that?" The Japanese, too, are steeped in history, yet they are also present-oriented and very good long-term planners. At present, there is no scientific explanation of why and how differences of this sort came about.

TIME AS COMMUNICATION

As surely as each culture has its spoken language, each has its own *language of time;* to function effectively in Japan you must learn the Japanese language of time. We each take our own time system for granted and project it onto other cultures. When this happens, we fail to read the hidden messages in the foreign time system, and thereby deny ourselves vital feedback.

Time is a basic system of both communication and organization. For Americans, how appointment time is used reveals how people feel about each other, how significant their business is, and where they rank in the status system. Time can also be used as an especially powerful form of insult. Furthermore, because the rules are informal, they operate largely out-of-awareness and, as a consequence, are less subject to conscious manipulation than language. It is important, therefore, to know how to read the messages associated with time in other cultures. In Japan, appointments and scheduling are handled according to M-time rules, whereas almost everything else is polychronic. It is important to be on time in Japan for every appointment, particularly for golf games.

Tempo, Rhythm, and Synchrony

The other side of time, which is even less tangible—but no less important—is the rhythmic aspect. Because nature's cycles are rhythmic, it is understandable that rhythm and tempo might be two distinguishing features of any culture. Rhythm ties the people of a culture together, yet it can also isolate them from members of other cultures. In some cultures people move very slowly; in others, they move rapidly. When two such cultures meet, they are apt to have difficulty relating because they are not "in sync." This is important because synchrony—the subtle ability to move together—is vital to all collaborative efforts, be they conferring, administering, working together on machines, or even buying and selling.

People who move at a fast tempo are often perceived as "tailgating" those who move more slowly, and tailgating doesn't contribute to harmonious interaction. Nor does forcing fast-paced people to move too slowly. Americans complain that the Japanese take forever to reach decisions. Japanese complain that Americans do not respect their process of reaching consensus, which requires much more time than decision-making in America. Like the tonal scale of Japanese music, Japanese time is out of phase with American time, and vice versa. One has to be contexted to what is going on, because there will be times when everything seems to be at a standstill while actually a lot may be going on behind the scenes. Then there will be other times when everything moves at lightning speed and the American has to, figuratively, stand aside so he won't get in the way.

Scheduling and Lead Time

To be able to conduct business in an orderly manner, it is essential to know how much lead time is required for each activity, how far ahead to request an appointment, when it is too late to do so, how far ahead to schedule meetings or vacations, and how much time to allow for the preparation of a major report. In the United States, schedules are sacred; in Japan, scheduling cannot be initiated until meetings are held at all levels within the organization to permit essential discussions. Input from everyone is solicited and eventually a consensus is reached. Once consensus is reached, Japanese expect immediate action.

The system works well within Japan, but there are complications whenever overseas partners or participants are involved, most of whom have scheduled their own activities up to two years in advance. Lead time is itself a communication as well as an element in organization.

Lead time varies from culture to culture. In the United States, lead time can be read as an index of the relative importance of the business to be conducted, as well as of the status of the individuals concerned. Short lead time means that the business is of little importance; the longer the lead time, the greater the value of the proceedings. In some countries, two weeks is the minimum advance time for requesting appointments, while in Arab countries two weeks may be too long—a date set so far in advance "slides off their minds." For Arabs, three or four days may be preferable. In Japan lead time is usually much shorter than in the United States. It is difficult to say how many conferences on important subjects, attended by all the most competent and prestigious Japanese leaders in their field, fail to get suitable counterparts from the United States because of the short lead time. Although what happens is a blameless artifact of the way the two systems work, these accidents of culture are seldom understood.

Another instance is the matter of setting a date to end something. Americans schedule how long they will be in Japan for a series of meetings. *This is a mistake.* To keep from being under the psychological pressure of arriving at a decision by a particular date, be flexible. In this instance, the Japanese are very aware of the American pressure of being "under the gun," and use it to their advantage during negotiations.

The Importance of Proper Timing

Choosing the correct timing of an important event is crucial. Politicians stake their careers on it. In government and business alike, announcements of major changes or new programs must be carefully timed. The significance of different time segments of the day also has to be considered. Almost everywhere, certain times of the day, month, or year are reserved for certain activities and are not ordinarily interchangeable: regular time off from the job, vacations, and meal times, for example. In general, for northern European cultures, anything that occurs very early in the morning or late at night (that is, outside business hours) suggests an emergency. In Japan, there are also propitious and nonpropitious times; the system is sufficiently complex that it is wise to seek the advice of a local expert. In America, the short business lunch is common and the business dinner rare; this is not so in Japan, where the function of the business lunch and dinner is to create the proper atmosphere and get acquainted. Relaxing with business clients after work is crucial to building the close rapport that is absolutely necessary if one is to do business in Japan. Evenings are reserved for socializing with business partners and clients.

Appointments and Keeping People Waiting

How people treat time conveys how they regard the business or the person with whom they are dealing. Waiting time, for example, carries strong messages. In the United States you do not expect to be kept waiting—only people of very high status can keep people waiting without causing overt resentment. Having to wait is not only demeaning for Americans, but also indicates a lack of organization as well as lack of consideration for others.

Interactions between monochronic and polychronic people can be stressful unless both parties know and can decode the meanings behind each other's time system. For example, we were once involved in a research project in New Mexico, conducting interviews with Hispanics. Our subjects were sixth- or seventh-generation descendants of the original Spanish families who settled in North America in the early seventeenth century. Despite constant contact with Anglo-Saxon Americans for well over a hundred years, most Hispanics remain polychronic. In three summers of interviewing we never once achieved our goal of five interviews each week for each interviewer. We were lucky to have two or three. Appointments were forgotten or rearranged at the last minute. Interviews in Hispanic homes or offices were constantly interrupted when families came to visit or a friend dropped by. The Hispanics seemed to be juggling half a dozen activities simultaneously, even while the interviews were in progress.

Since we are monochronic Anglo-Saxons, this caused us no little concern and considerable distress. It is hard not to respond viscerally when your own time system is violated. Our intellectual understanding of the monochronic/polychronic time differences did not mitigate our feelings of frustration; we did recognize, however, that what we were experiencing was a consequence of cultural differences and was, therefore, a part of our data. This led us to a better understanding of the importance of information flow and information networks in a polychronic society.

If an American responds to a foreign time system as if it were his own, he does so at his own risk. The meaning of being late, being kept waiting, or missing appointments in a polychronic culture is simply not the same as it is in the United States.

INFORMATION FLOW:
IS IT FAST OR SLOW
AND WHERE DOES IT GO?

 Information flow is measured by how long it takes a message calling for an action to travel from one part of an organization to another and for that message to be acted on. How information flows in a culture may be the single most important thing for the outsider to learn, since cultural differences in information flow are often the greatest stumbling blocks to international understanding. Every executive doing business in a foreign land should know how information is handled—where it goes, and whether it flows easily through the society and the business organization, or whether it is restricted to narrow channels due to compartmentalization.

Information flow is a concept which may seem nebulous and abstract at first; it will only become apparent to those who have conditioned themselves to look for it. Its results, however, are quite easily seen. In some cultures, such as the Japanese and Spanish, information spreads rapidly and moves almost as if it had a life of its own. In other countries, such as the United States, Germany, and Switzerland, information is highly focused, compartmentalized, and not apt to flow freely. Those who use information as an instrument of "command and control" and who build their planning on controlling information are in for a rude shock in Japan, where there are no secrets. Different strategies are required, and executives are well advised to adapt to the rapid flow of information rather than to try to control its flow the way we do in the United States. Clearly this calls for a complete revamping of all information strategies—both internal and external.

In high-context cultures, where people are spatially in volved with each other, information flows freely. As people are already highly contexted and therefore don't need to be briefed in much detail for each transaction, the emphasis is on stored rather than on transmitted information. Furthermore, channels are seldom overloaded because people stay in constant contact. Schedules and screening (as in the use of private offices) are avoided because they interfere with this vital contact. Interpersonal contacts take precedence over everything else. There are two primary functions of a Japanese meeting and, therefore, two primary expectations: (1) to context everybody, in order to open up the information channels and determine whether the group can work together; and (2) to appraise the chances of coming to an agreement in the future.

In high-flow information cultures, being out of touch means that essentially one ceases to exist. This is experienced by high-context Japanese who are overseas for long periods and who recognize the crucial importance of keeping in touch. These Japanese make every effort to return home frequently enough to maintain their place in people's minds and to keep themselves up to date on the latest information.

Low-flow organizations are familiar to both Americans and northern Europeans because low-flow information is associated with both low context and monochronic time; they occur as a result not only of taking up one thing at a time, but of the compartmentalization associated with LC institutions.

The authors were once hired as consultants to a large government bureaucracy in which there was a good deal of dissatisfaction. As would be expected, there were multiple causes, the most important of which was a bottleneck created by a high-ranking bureaucrat that blocked practically everything going from the top down and from bottom up. Once the problem had been identified, one of the agency director's staff remarked, "I see we have a blockage in information." In a high-flow, high-context situation everyone would have already known that this was the case. In a low-flow system, however, it was necessary to call in outside consultants to make explicit what some people suspected but were unable to pin down.

ACTION CHAINS:
THE IMPORTANCE OF COMPLETION

友 An action chain is an established sequence of events in which one or more people participate— and contribute—to achieve a goal. It's like the old-fashioned ritual of courtship with its time-honored developmental stages. If either party rushes things too much, omits an important procedure, or delays too long between steps, the courtship grinds to a halt. Action chains cover a wide range of events: mergers and takeovers, setting up joint enterprises or a new division, hiring and training personnel, and even an individual's train of thought.

Business is replete with action chains: greeting people, training salesmen, developing an advertising campaign, floating a stock offering, initiating a lawsuit, or even sinking a golf putt. Many bureaucratic procedures are based unconsciously on the action-chain model. Because of the diversity of these functions, it may be difficult for some people to link these activities in their minds, but it is the common thread of underlying, ordered sequence that ties each case to the others.

Because the steps in the chain are either highly technical, as in floating a stock offering or completing a merger, or else so widely shared and taken for granted that little conscious attention is paid to the details, the tremendous need to reexamine the entire pattern is seldom recognized in the overseas setting.

Some important rules govern the structure, though not the content, of action chains, and these rules vary from group to group. For example, if an important step is left out, the action must begin all over again. Or, too many meetings and reports can break action chains, making it difficult for people to complete their work. In fact, the breaking of an action chain is one of the most troublesome events with which human beings have to contend in our speeded-up, technical twentieth century.

Cultures can be arranged along a continuum, from those in which motivation to complete a job (what the psychologists call "closure") is minimal to those in which motivation to finish tasks is very strong. All planning must take into account this elaborate hierarchy of action chains. Monochronic, low-context cultures, with their compartmentalized approach and depending as they do on scheduled activities, are particularly sensitive to interruptions. They are, therefore, more vulnerable to the breaking of action chains than high-context cultures. In general, the higher the context, the more stable the system and the lower its vulnerability to such breaks. High-context people, because of their intense involvement with each other and their extensive, cohesive networks, are more elastic; there is more "give" in their system. Some polychronic people will break an action chain simply because they don't like the way things are going or because they think they can "get a better deal." For instance, we once knew a monochronic architect in New York who was designing a building for some polychronic clients. Her clients were continually changing the specifications for the building as they had new ideas or perceived their own needs differently, even down to requesting changes in the building's foundations. Designing and constructing a building is an elaborate collection of action chains. Interruptions and changes of the type experienced by this architect can be devastating in their consequences. When the Japanese break action chains, it can be very unsettling to Americans, because Americans are brought up with a strong drive to complete action chains.

The relationship between action chains and disputes is important. Even though they may not always work, all cultures have built-in safeguards to prevent disputes from escalating to an out-and-out battle. Keep in mind, however, that these safeguards apply only within the context of the culture. In any situation where a dispute appears imminent, it is essential to do two things immediately: proceed slowly, taking every action possible to maintain course and stay on an even keel; and seek the advice of a skillful, subtle interpreter of the culture.

INTERFACING:
COMMUNICATING ONE ON ONE

友 The concept of interfacing can be illustrated by a simple example: it is impossible to interface an American appliance with a European outlet without an adapter and a transformer. Not only are the voltages different, but the contacts on one are round, on the other thin and flat. The purpose of this book is to serve as an adapter for business executives operating at the interface between American and Japanese cultures.

The problems to be solved when interfacing vary from company to company, but a few generalizations are possible. First, it is more difficult to succeed in a foreign country than at home. Second, the top management of a foreign subsidiary is crucial to the success of interfacing. Therefore, it is important to send the very best people available, take their advice, and leave them alone. Learn to expect that your Japanese manager or representative will start explaining things in terms of the "Japanese mentality," which may sound somewhat alien and strange.

Cultural interfacing follows five basic principles:

1. The higher the context of either the culture or the industry, the more difficult the interface

2. The greater the complexity of the elements, the more difficult the interface
3. The greater the cultural distance, the more difficult the interface
4. The greater the number of levels in the system, the more difficult the interface
5. Very simple, low-context, highly evolved, mechanical systems tend to produce fewer interface problems than multiple-level systems of great complexity that depend on human talent for their success

An example of an *easy-to-interface* business would be the manufacture of small components for microscopes by two divisions, one in Germany, the other in Switzerland. The cultural distance in this case is not great since both cultures are low-context as well as monochronic, and the business operation itself does not involve different levels of complexity.

A *difficult-to-interface* enterprise would be a newspaper or magazine in two countries that are not that different, such as Germany and the United States. Publishing is a high-context enterprise which must be neatly meshed at literally dozens of points, including writing, advertising, and editorial policy. The success of newspapers and magazines depends on writers and editors who understand their audience's culture and know how to reach their readers.

An *extremely-difficult-to-interface* enterprise would be a magazine, periodical, newspaper, or TV enterprise headquartered in either America or Japan with a regular publication schedule in the other country. The cultural distance is enormous. The United States is low-context and monochronic, while Japan is high-context and polychronic. Japan is homogeneous, while the United States is regional and multi-ethnic. Japan is an island, the United States is a continent. The United States is relatively sparsely populated, while Japan packs 120 million people into a fraction of the area of our country. Such an enterprise requires great sophistication and flexibility at the top in order to succeed.

SUMMARY

友 In organizations, everything management does communicates; when viewed in the cultural context, all acts, all events, all material things have meaning. Some organizations send strong, consistent messages that are readily grasped by employees and customers alike. Other organizations are less easy to interpret; they do not communicate clearly, or their messages are incongruent. Sometimes one part of the organization communicates one thing and another part communicates something else. The cues around which these corporate and cultural messages are organized are as different as the languages with which they are associated. Most important, their meaning is deeply imbedded and therefore harder for management to change when making the transition from the United States to Japan.

Speed of messages, contexts, space, time, information flow, action chains, and interfacing are all involved in the creation of both national and corporate character. This book is organized to help the American reader understand the subtlety and complexity of culture as well as the interrelation of its parts.

Part II 吉

THE JAPANESE

INTRODUCTION

友 The study of the history of the human race teaches us that technology, science, philosophy, and religion have all *evolved,* though not always at the same rate or even in harmony with each other. In most cases the evolution was slow at first and then progressed logarithmically. This is particularly true of technology. However, an evolutionary view contains within it at least two hidden traps. First, evolution implies a process in which the superior survive and therefore pass on to their offspring traits which become refined or more highly evolved. This process in turn leads to the belief that whatever is different or older is less highly evolved, a theory known as social Darwinism. And while there is a certain appeal to popular sentiment in the tradition of social Darwinism, the approach can distort one's view of the world; it has the further disadvantage of placing an intellectual block in the way of accepting anything that is outside one's own familiar culture.

The second invisible trap is that most people, whether they are aware of it or not, are resistant to change or to doing things differently. We Americans are particularly vulnerable on this score, in part because of our affluence and our past successes. Also, because we are a large and prosperous nation with no close neighbors who can seriously compete with us, many Americans grow up with the notion that we are simply the best in the world and have the answers to everything. This view, when applied to the Japanese, is counterproductive for at least three reasons: Japan has bested the United States in a number of commercial arenas; she has a long and illustrious past, and has made significant contributions to world culture; if one hopes to succeed in either the Japanese or the world market, a prime requisite is respect for one's partners as well as one's competitors.

The more one learns about relations with people like the Japanese, the more one is impressed with the power of the idea that the world's greatest and most valuable resource is people and the many different ways in which they mobilize energy through information.

HISTORICAL BACKGROUND:
CONTEXT FOR JAPAN TODAY

友 For Europeans and Americans, Japan has always been a paradoxical mix of the enigmatic and the exotic. Many Westerners feel there are many things about Japan that they will never understand. It is our theory that some of these enigmas result not so much from subtle, important cultural difficulties as from the Westerner's looking at the wrong things in the wrong places. A few words concerning Japanese history may be useful in orienting the Westerner to Japanese ways.

It has not been easy for foreigners to look beyond Japan's colorful and sometimes mysterious exterior in order to glean its deeper patterns and significance. Its religions are strikingly different from Western religions; its material culture has nearly mesmerized the outsider and has come to symbolize Japan to the West. Japanese art and calligraphy, geishas, *Noh* plays, the Kabuki theater, Buddhist temples, Confucianism, Shinto shrines, and, last but not least, the tradition of an emperor who was once revered as a living deity, are all aspects of a culture that has captured the attention and stimulated the imagination of the West. One could easily spend a lifetime learning about Japanese surface culture. Yet outward manifestations should not be confused with the basic underlying culture. In fact, these surface culture traits which appear so significant to us are like the carapace of the tortoise: they hide and protect the real Japan. Commodore Perry may have thought he "opened" Japan to the West; in fact, as with all cultures, what was revealed on the surface was little more than an illusion.

THE CASTLE AND THE VILLAGE

To understand the past properly as well as the present in Japan, it is necessary to take into account two separate currents in the stream of historical Japanese culture: the interdependent roles played by the feudal lord and the agricultural villages that sustained him. The influence of both can be seen beneath the surface wherever one looks in Japan.

The restoration of the *Meiji* line of emperors in 1867 signified two important events in Japanese history. It marked the end of Japan's protracted period of feudalism as well as the end of the shogunate, the leaders who had governed Japan in the name of the emperor. With the downfall of the shogunate came the demise of the deeply entrenched samurai, or warrior, class which had dominated that society for more than a thousand years. However, the shogunate and the system from which it evolved left an indelible stamp on Japan.

Beginning with the *Meiji* period (1868–1912) and Admiral Dewey's forced entry into the Japanese fortress, Japanese feudalism quite readily, and in a surprisingly short time, transformed itself via the mechanism of the great *zaibatsu* (consortium of large business firms) into its own version of twentieth-century industrialism—by keeping the spirit of the samurai alive in modern Japan.

Several aspects of the village tradition are evident as "ideals" in Japan's present-day culture. Among them are leisurely and task-oriented teamwork, which grew out of planting, cultivating, and harvesting rice; consensus decision-making; and equality among co-workers and members of the organizational family. The paradox here is that the Japanese appear to be very egalitarian in certain situations (when they work together as a team) and rigidly hierarchical in others. However, closer examination reveals ever-present, subtle but binding status distinctions. The hierarchy is always there.

One of the most important characteristics of the Japanese is their strong sense of group identity. This pervades every level of the society. Group ties are so strong that members feel a collective sense of responsibility for each other's actions.

LEADERSHIP: THE WARRIOR

While in the Western world the military man's role was commonly that of an adjunct or servant of religious, political, or economic institutions, in Japan the reverse has been true. For centuries, the warrior class in Japan was at the top, outranking all others. When Japan was stripped of the external, visible military trappings, it was still dominated internally by the pervasive spirit and structure of its military institutions.

Japanese society is organized and functions according to military tenets. We are referring to traits such as the strong hierarchical structure; insistence on following the chain of command; daily acknowledgment of differences in rank between individuals; an obsession with loyalty; deep personal attachments; emphasis on the performance of the group (a major contrast to European individualism); willingness to make both individual and group sacrifices to reach a major objective; strong feelings of identity with, and loyalty to, those within the group, in contrast to those who do not belong (clear-cut lines between insiders and outsiders); a belief that the organizational objective is the *raison d'être* for existence; and strategic ways of thinking (both in business and in government).

The reason the West doesn't do better in competition with Japan is that it is competing with a society that doesn't conduct business, but rather *wages* business—with the intensity and concentration with which it might wage war. Conversely, only a small proportion of the Western world, European or American, consists of warriors at heart. Perhaps this explains why in our interviews the successful American and European business executives who really seemed to understand the Japanese and who felt at ease dealing with them frequently had a history of military service. It is interesting to note that, while military men are not known for their flexibility of mind, they do for the most part pay very close attention to the way in which the opposition fights.

What makes the Japanese system work so well is the manner in which leadership and decision-making are structured. There has never been any doubt in the Japanese mind as to who is in charge. Possibly because they are so confident and secure, Japanese leaders are usually loath to throw their weight around. Proving that one is the boss becomes unnecessary. One doesn't even have to give orders in the American style. It is up to one's subordinates to work things out, and subordinates know they will be rated on how well they perform. Everyone in the organization is informed and has par-

[handwritten note in top-left corner]

in the decision-making process in all matters con-
he welfare and future of the organization.

The military metaphor should give the American CEO a
familiar conceptual tool in dealing with the complexity he will
meet in Japan. At the same time the reader must understand
that a knowledge of the American military will not automatically render the Japanese system accessible. The Japanese
military is built on unique traditions and patterns, some of
which have been in place since the beginning of medieval
times. Still, the metaphor may help to explain, for example,
why it is that Japanese managers of foreign subsidiaries are
given unbridled latitude and authority to make critical decisions on their own. From this perspective it is possible to see
that "headquarters" can't have the general staff interfering
with its field commanders.

MODERN JAPAN

ORDER AND RANK

[handwritten note in left margin]

"There is no situation as awkward in Japan as when the
appropriate order is ignored or broken."

Chie Nakane, *Japanese Society*

The relation of leadership to the group pervades
everything the Japanese do; the result is a vertical
social organization. Important relationships are
within the individual's immediate group: his family and his

business or professional group, the people he works with every day.

The organizing principle for Japanese society is ranking rather than stratification. Therefore, it is important to learn some of the signs of rank and how to interpret them. During a conference, the highest-ranking individual at a table often sits farthest from the door; at other times he may sit at the middle, surrounded by lower-ranking associates. While waiting for his host, the visitor sits in the chair facing the door where his host will enter. In a group, the person of highest rank walks slightly in front, goes through the door first, and sits down first. Other subtle signs of rank are clothes that are conservative and well-tailored and a bearing and manner that communicate restrained power, poise, and politeness.

In the words of Thomas Rohlen, in his book about the social organization of a Japanese bank, *For Harmony and Strength,* "Close attention to the implications of behavior and the arrangement of groups allows those with a practised eye to perceive differences in rank readily." For the Japanese, order depends on people's knowing and accepting their proper place or rank and on not disturbing the "proper order" of things. This insures harmonious interaction, one of the Japanese's highest priorities.

It is also very important for Americans to know that formality should govern one's relations with the Japanese. Informality is perceived as rudeness. They dislike intensely the use of first names and the American penchant for back-slapping and attempts to be "buddies." All of these are viewed as insulting and unwarranted familiarity.

The American occupation after World War II imposed its own definition of order on the Japanese by eliminating patterns that it considered antithetical to personal freedom, such as the ironbound authority of the head of the household over the whole family. However, there still remains a vast reser-

voir of behavior, institutions, and organizational patterns that
are deeply rooted in traditional Japanese culture. To illustrate:

◄ ◄ ► ►

A very successful European businessman with more than a
quarter century of experience with the Japanese awoke one
morning to find his company incapacitated by a strike. To
save his business, he immediately called in the best labor
experts. Their report was a dossier of all the classic mistakes
that one can make when applying one's own unwritten rules
and concepts of order to a foreign culture. The report identified numerous errors ranging from inadequate personnel
screening to gross mishandling of how information and orders to subordinates were channeled. In effect, the rules
governing the basic order of Japanese life (and business) had
been violated. Chief among these was failure to follow the
Japanese chain of command. The European businessman had
assumed that since he owned the company he had the right
to skip channels and give instructions directly to any employee. He said: "I really learned that you have to pay attention to rank, the *honbucho, bucho,* and *kacho.* If you ignore
them, everything stops. Now I go by their rules." *(Honbucho,
bucho,* and *kacho* roughly translate into general manager,
division manager, and section manager.)

◄ ◄ ► ►

Rules of order must be followed everywhere, especially at
the highest levels of government and diplomacy. In world
affairs, the Japanese are very conscious of their position as a
nation. They do not take kindly any implication that they are
not a first-class world power. Some Americans and Europeans have indulged themselves by patronizing the Japanese, a
monumental mistake.

THE FAMILY: ABSENT FATHER, OMNIPOTENT MOTHER

Japanese children, especially boys, are brought up permissively; and the bond between mother and child is strong. The indulgence of the mother creates extreme dependence. The Japanese mother sees her child as an extension of herself and thus sets the stage for lifelong dependency relationships.

During his early years the Japanese child begins to understand that his performance and behavior will be considered a direct reflection of his love for his mother. Any failure will cause her great pain and make the child feel guilty. The mother becomes his coach and tutor; the Japanese term is *kyoiku-mama,* which means "education mama." If he does well, she's proud; if he fails, she is disgraced. The fear of causing her pain or even disappointment is so great that the child is always spurred to greater efforts (see Garfinkel, "The Best Jewish Mother in the World," in the Reading List).

In her book *Japanese Women,* Takie Sugiyama Lebra describes the training young girls receive at home that instills cultural values and conditions them to proper comportment. These values include modesty, reticence, elegance in handling such things as chopsticks and dishes, tidiness, courtesy, compliance, discipline for self-reliance, diligence, endurance, and a willingness to work around the house. Japanese girls are groomed to be skilled wives and mothers.

With her husband working long hours and seldom being at home, the Japanese wife often feels abandoned when her children grow up and she no longer has responsibility for their education. Many wives suffer from depression; some have nervous breakdowns, others turn to alcohol. Unfortunately, it is difficult in Japan for middle-aged women to find employment, and since they have usually been raised to be wives

and mothers they have little experience or education to prepare them for work outside the home.

TERRITORIALITY:
CROWDING WITHOUT CONTACT

Most Americans are conditioned to avoid close physical
contact and generally observe the northern European pattern
of "keeping their distance." They tend to stand and sit much
farther apart than the Japanese, who will endure crowd conditions in public that most Americans would find intolerable,
especially on subways and commuter trains. Nevertheless, in
social and formal situations, polite Japanese try to avoid acci-
dental touching and guard against any sign of spatial intimacy. It is important to remember that any violation of spatial
patterns is experienced personally. In shaking hands with
Japanese, avoid a hard grip; they neither like nor respect
"bone crunchers."

As noted earlier, American business favors private offices,
which are status symbols. In some American firms there is an
open-door policy to facilitate communication and ready access. In Japan, most executives favor sharing offices to insure
that information is shared so that each knows what is happening in the others' areas of responsibility. Again, it's the sea of
information that is vital to the Japanese. In Japanese firms
there are ceremonial rooms for receiving visitors and for
special meetings, but normally there are no other work areas
that afford real privacy.

Traditionally, in Japanese homes there is little privacy as
Americans think of it. The Japanese often live in very
crowded conditions, especially in large cities, where the rents
are very high (the average size of Japanese family housing is
282 square feet). In earlier times, paper walls (no longer
common) screened sight but not sound from the other rooms,

from neighbors, or from the street. Lacking auditory privacy, the Japanese have learned to tolerate loud noises, even the blare of loudspeakers from demonstrators. The American in Japan must find a way to cope with the distractions of auditory intrusions.

In Japanese homes there is an important distinction between the inside and the outside of a house or apartment. One always removes one's overcoat before entering a house or office. The outside area includes the entryway, where visitors remove their shoes, as visitors should always do before entering a Japanese home (usually the host will provide slippers). Inside there is a floor covering called *tatami,* a very fine straw matting, and one never walks on *tatami* with shoes.

EDUCATION: CONFORMITY IN THE CLASSROOM

"Japanese achievement motivation, which is very high, is based not on training for independence and self-reliance as in the West, but rather on the instilling of affiliative and dependency needs."

Robert J. Smith, *Japanese Society*

◄◄►►

Japanese students are among the best-educated in the world. Japan has an illiteracy rate of less than 1 percent compared to the United States' rate of 8 percent. Ninety-nine percent of Japanese students complete high school, compared to 80 percent of American students. Also, it should be noted that there are 240 days of school per year in Japan compared to 180 in the United States. The Japanese educational system has produced students who consistently score high on standardized tests administered to high school students in twenty industrialized countries. In a recent article in *Science,* "Mathematics Achievement of Chinese, Japanese, and American Children," by Stevenson, Lee, and Stigler (see Reading List), the authors state: "Although a small proportion of American children perform superbly, the large majority appear to be falling behind their peers in other countries." The authors attribute this gap to complacency on the part of American parents, who do not see a need for improvement in part because they are unaware of the high performance of children in other countries.

From the close, dependent relationship at home the Japanese child enters school to find a highly competitive atmosphere where excellence and achievement are stressed. He reaches out to the group to satisfy his yearning for dependence and at the same time he is under enormous pressure to compete. Quite often his mother arranges after-school tutoring *(juku* school) and she also tutors him herself at home. The price exacted in terms of pressure to excel has been devastating to some students.

High school pressures culminate in "examination hell," the time when students all over the country must compete for admission to the prestigious universities. There is widespread concern about the effects of this intense competition and the negative impact on many adolescents. Many of them become ill, some suffer breakdowns and depression, and a few even commit suicide if they do not do well on examinations. Another factor which weighs heavily on adolescents is the frequent absence of the father, whose long working hours prevent his spending much time with his family.

Japanese critics complain that the educational system relies too much on rote learning and discourages independent thinking. There is now talk of reform to make the system more responsive to individual differences and abilities as well as to reduce the pressure on students.

As one might predict in a society where everything is ranked, schools, colleges, and universities are also ranked. The old Imperial University, now called Tokyo University *(Todai),* is at the top, and its graduates form an influential network that penetrates virtually every power center in Japan. With rewards such as these in mind, Japanese mothers do everything they can to get their sons on the right track academically and into the best universities.

One of the first things Japanese communities overseas do is start a Japanese school. This insures their children an opportunity to keep up with their classmates at home so that when they return to Japan they can continue on their path toward acceptance by one of the good universities.

The bond between school classmates extends throughout life and includes all levels of education, grade school through university. Classmates occupy a special status in one's circle of friends and acquaintances. One is obligated to give them special consideration and assistance regardless of the level of personal friendship.

THE YOUNGER GENERATION TODAY: LOOSENING UP

As in so many countries today, the older generation in Japan is worried about the decay in traditional values and the lack of a strong work ethic in the younger generation. It is not uncommon for Japanese adolescents to act out their repressed anxiety and hostility against teachers and other authority figures. Some students revolt against the system. The older generation is becoming increasingly concerned by the fact that middle-class Japanese families often raise their children in affluence, providing for all their material needs; quite often the children, overprotected and indulged, are unsure of themselves and their goals and lack a sense of responsibility

and purpose in life. A number of thoughtful Japanese voiced
their concern about the future of the country and, in particular, their fears about the future of business. We were told that
some young Japanese are much less interested in working
hard than their parents were. Some of the more sophisticated
and experienced Japanese business executives fear that what
has happened in Europe will happen in Japan. One Japanese
executive made this observation:

> "We must never forget that behind the great suc-
> cess of German business in the world market lie
> many years of hard work. They struggled for years
> to rebuild their industry after the war and they
> worked very hard to achieve their success. Now
> they are becoming spoiled. Perhaps there is a les-
> son here for all of us."

THE SEA OF INFORMATION

The Japanese are avid readers. There are twenty-seven
thousand bookstores in Japan, about the same number as in
the entire United States, and they are usually filled with eager
customers. Japanese newspapers have a daily circulation of
34 million in a country of 120 million. The average Japanese
family watches television approximately five hours a day,
and, in contrast to entertainment-oriented American television programming, Japanese programming is approximately
75 percent news, cultural events, and education, and only 25
percent entertainment. It's no wonder they are well informed.

On the job the average American needs a great deal of
information about exactly what is expected of him. He needs
procedures and explicit directions. The Japanese doesn't
need procedures because he is expected to inform himself.

Since he is very high-context, he expects other people to be similarly contexted—informed about everything, including procedures. The Japanese needs are for information about human relationships, feedback on how things are going and how people are feeling.

Many Japanese business executives are very well informed about American culture; before they start working in the United States, they read extensively from books, articles, and reports, both general and technical. For example, many Japanese business executives and government officials are well versed in the workings of the American political system. One American banker had this to say:

> "The Japan lobby on Capitol Hill is one of the strongest and best-connected lobbies in Washington. They know all the key congressional legislative assistants, follow the drafts of legislation affecting Japan, provide input and advice at every stage of legislation, and they rally political and financial power to pressure Congress. In 1984 Japan spent three million dollars on lobbyists. They have the best lobbyists in the business."

THE VOCABULARY
OF HUMAN RELATIONSHIPS

友 Knowledge of the meaning of a number of key Japanese terms makes it possible to understand some of the heretofore hidden features of Japanese psychology and culture. One of the strengths of modern science is a shared agreement as to the meaning of scientific words and symbols; if there were no agreement, unified science would be impossible. To understand the Japanese, Americans must learn some new terms, words whose equivalents do not exist in English; these words have immediate and profound meanings to the Japanese, but would require volumes to be explained fully to Americans. These terms are very high on the context scale and constitute vital elements in the vocabulary of human relationships in Japan; they are well worth the effort required to appreciate their meaning.

"AMAE"

We begin with the term *amae,* a word with many meanings and varied connotations depending on the context. The closest English word is "dependency," but dependency in the United States has a negative connotation that it does not have in Japan. *Amae is the glue that holds Japanese society together.*

Amae means feelings of closeness and dependency, the emotions an infant feels for its mother. These emotions and the needs they engender continue to operate throughout the Japanese lifespan. The loyalty that is felt between members of a work force is strengthened by *amae* among the group. A Japanese male, when embarking upon a career, will knowingly enter into a dependency relationship with men of power, status, and influence. This binds him to them in a reciprocal relationship (the reciprocal term, *amaeru,* means "to depend on the affection of another"), and while he benefits from the favors (which must be repaid, of course) it is the emotional tie that is important to him.

Americans will find it difficult to understand how a man could actively seek dependence on another man. Our cultural currents (for males) run in the opposite direction—toward *independence.* Yet the *amae* syndrome is entirely consistent with other dominant themes in Japanese life. The Japanese find it easier to communicate with another human being if they are in a dependency relationship with that person.

The larger Japanese companies reflect *amae* in their relationship to employees by providing health and life insurance, housing for some employees and housing allowances for others, low-interest mortgage rates, vacation facilities, weekend retreats, athletic facilities and team equipment, and education and training both in-house and at technical schools and universities. In return, employees identify closely with the company, which gradually becomes at least as important as their family. Employees depend on the company just as the company depends on its employees.

The crucial point about *amae* is that one's personal identity is rooted in the soil of one's dependent and interdependent relations to others as a *member of a group.* In contrast, the

American and the European seeks his identity not as a cog in a larger machine but as an individual. Not only must he free himself from his parents but also he must maintain some distance from all groups, even if he is a member of the group. For Westerners, being too closely identified with a group is tantamount to *giving up one's identity*. Herein lies the greatest distinction between Japanese and Americans. (For further information about *amae*, we refer the reader to Dr. Takeo Doi's insightful book, *The Anatomy of Dependence*.)

Strong drives to conform characterize the Japanese. The Japanese child is encouraged to conform at home as well as in school, where he is rigidly programmed; a child who tries to deviate from the prescribed lesson will be quickly brought back into line. As in calligraphy, there is one right way to do everything; nothing else is allowed.

In adult life, Japanese conformity focuses on the "reference group," the group with which one works in a company. Loyalty to the group is felt to be one of life's highest values and is the principal means by which an employee's worth is measured. Conformity is a strong and dependable indicator of the individual's loyalty.

Two important differences spring from the soil of Japanese group identity: privacy for the individual is not important, and since the "public" is outside one's group, the Japanese have little of what Americans call "public spirit." To the Japanese the concept of individual freedom does not have the same value it has in the United States. To understand and appreciate such apparent contradictions, one must be able to "jump over one's shadow," as one of our respondents phrased it.

"GIRI" AND "ON"

Closely related to *amae* is *giri*, which means one's indebtedness to others, past and present. A sense of indebtedness is ever present in Japanese society, and the concept of *giri* includes one's ancestors and all those who have gone before as well as one's contemporaries. In every relationship one feels the strong need to fulfill responsibilities.

On is the term for obligations, from minor matters to major concerns. It involves giving and granting favors, again with a burden of indebtedness. A Japanese feels special lifelong obligations to his teachers and his bosses, past and present. The passage of time never weakens this obligation. If anything, it results in even greater feelings of indebtedness.

Giri and *on* begin in infancy and are carried within the individual throughout his lifetime. How well one discharges one's responsibility is part of one's *kao* (face). English has no term comparable to *kao*. *Kao* encompasses pride, self-esteem, and reputation. It is vital to the Japanese. A foreigner should avoid criticizing a Japanese or demeaning him in any way, nor should one disparage his work. All of these actions are considered anathema.

A strong desire to maintain harmony characterizes the Japanese. They are very concerned about other people's feelings. They hate to say "No." Instead, they say, "I will consider your request very carefully." Americans often complain that Japanese lead them to believe they agree to something which, it later turns out, they reject. Remember, when you ask for something, the Japanese avoid saying no, even though that's what they mean. You must therefore learn to read the subtle signs of a negative reaction. (We refer the reader to Masaaki Imai's book, *16 Ways to Avoid Saying No.*)

Since saving face is very important to the Japanese, they do not criticize and they hate to make a mistake. You don't hear Japanese saying, "I told you that wouldn't work." The Japanese do not understand people who criticize their own country or their company. They consider this extremely disloyal. Be warned—if you do this, you will lose face.

"NINGEN KANKEI"

"If Japanese society is seen as a network of inter-locking relationships, hierarchically arranged, the strands of that net are formed by *ningen kankei.*"

Mark Zimmerman, *How to Do Business with the Japanese*

◄◄►►

Ningen kankei involves closeness and cooperation between people in mutually beneficial relationships which spring from a variety of sources. In addition to former classmates it includes people who come from the same town or who are working for the same company. All of these shared experiences create special bonds between people that are part of *ningen kankei.* These relationships are carefully tended over long periods of time. *Ningen kankei* furthers the goals of those involved and is reinforced by feelings of duty and obligation and sometimes genuine friendship.

Employees of the same organization tend to form *ningen kankei* with people of their same level but in different parts of the company (those in the same department might be in competition). *Ningen kankei* is greatly strengthened by after-hours socializing in bars or on the golf course over the weekend.

As a foreigner develops contacts among the Japanese he would be well advised to keep his contacts informed on all matters of interest to them. In all likelihood the Japanese will reciprocate and the foreigner can start building his own all-important information networks. One never knows when a new acquaintance will prove useful. Our advice is try to build as many relationships as possible and remember that acts of thoughtfulness and kindness will be repaid many times over.

Cultivating relationships requires time; one starts slowly and spends a great deal of time learning about the background of people who might be helpful in order to be contexted to their interests and needs.

Most important, remember that these relationships are based on genuine good feeling, not exploitation. One gives and one receives from the heart.

But do not expect that, once you know them, your Japanese friends will then behave like Americans. The Japanese hide their emotions, and are very restrained in showing feelings. As one Japanese observed, "We share our sorrows and we hide delight." When Japanese are complimented or congratulated, they look abashed or embarrassed, which is confusing to Americans, who expect them to smile and look happy.

As a corollary to *ningen kankei,* the Japanese distrust verbal facility because they believe it denotes superficiality. They communicate their true inner feelings by innuendo and nonverbal means. Chie Nakane, the distinguished Japanese anthropologist and author of the classic *Japanese Society,* gives a perfect example of a high-context interaction in her description of a Japanese dealing with his own group:

> ". . . members of the group know each other exceedingly well. One's family life, love affairs, even the limits of one's capacity for cocktails are intimately known to others. Among fellow members a single word would suffice for the whole sentence. The mutually sensitive response goes so far that each easily recognizes the other's slightest change in behavior and mood and is ready to react accordingly."

OTHER HIGH-CONTEXT TERMS

There are many other important terms in the Japanese
vocabulary of human relationships. The list that follows suggests several things: first, a lesson that Americans seem to
need to learn again and again—namely, that HC systems, by
virtue of the fact that context is widely shared, are systems of
great and deep involvement of the participants with each
other. The closest analogue most people know is that of twins
who have grown up together or people who have been
through a great deal together over a long period of time. In
this sense, it is sometimes convenient to think of Japan as a
very large family with the emperor as the head of that family.
Second, shared information means not only high involvement but also many ways of talking about the subtlety of that
involvement. The shared behavior patterns inherent in these
concepts make the Japanese sensitive to even the subtlest of
changes in emotional tone. They are sensitive to feedback
from friends and colleagues, and their awareness of nuances
of response in the marketplace makes American marketing
analyses seem crude. Third, as there are insiders, there are
also outsiders and specified emotions and commitments (or
lack thereof) for dealing with them. Japanese can be ruthless
with outsiders. Therefore, it is not surprising that the Japanese
are considered ethnocentric. We heard many accounts of
discrimination against foreigners, Asians as well as Westerners of all nationalities. The use of the term *tanin* is significant:
"other persons" roughly translates to "nonpersons." Unless
the visiting businessperson is a tourist with nothing at stake, it
is dangerous to maintain the status of *tanin*. In Japan, connections and friends are imperative.

Some important additional high-context Japanese terms:

haragei   belly language; nonverbal communication to convey true intentions

jibun   one's self; awareness of self

enryo   special consideration for another, taking into account the fact that by holding back part of oneself one may not satisfy needs for *amae* (dealing with Americans requires *enryo* for most Japanese)

kao   face; personal honor

kimochi   feelings (very important, even in business)

nemawashi   preparing the groundwork

ninjo   ability to read and experience feelings of others

omote   front; the face or image one presents to others (one is "on guard")

ura   back; real feelings (one is "off guard"); related to *tatemae* and *honne;* see below

tatemae   front face; what is presented

honne   true feelings privately held *(tatemae* and *honne* are interdependent)

uchi   inside; insider; member of group

soto   outside; outsider; not one of the group

wa   harmony (vital)

Part III 吉

JAPANESE BUSINESS

CORPORATE PHILOSOPHY

THE TEAM AND THE WORK ETHIC

友 Each major Japanese business has a philosophy that permeates its organization and is taken very seriously. This philosophy is often based on the Confucian ideal of serving society and showing respect for law, ceremonies, and community relationships. For example, each spring company presidents talk to new recruits, some of them graduates of the best universities, who are inducted into the company with great ceremony and solemnity. Company presidents usually stress the importance of personal growth, the need to work for the common good of society, the need for consensus, building good human relationships, and working in harmony with the group. For the individual employee, loyalty is most important. The president is sure to remind new recruits, called "freshmen," that there is more to business than making money.

In our opinion, neither management skills nor corporate philosophy is ultimately responsible for the phenomenal success of Japanese business. Rather, the success grows out of the strong Confucian and Buddhist work ethic that pervades management and labor, and out of the group orientation that is fostered in the educational system. These two traits are reinforced by the pervasive influence of Japanese culture in family life and education. In the words of Jared Taylor in *Shadows of the Rising Sun:*

"It is the Japanese worker, not the executive, who
has made Japan great. . . . Management's main
achievement is to have channeled the qualities that
workers bring to their job in the first place."

We would add that management's achievement also lies in
its recognition and encouragement of those qualities, and in
its skill in developing them.

JOINING A MAJOR COMPANY

After being hired by a major company, each employee
signs a contract which is the essence of simplicity by American standards. The contract states that the person is a member of the company and that he pledges to follow the company rules. The contract has no details about rights, duties,
procedures, redress, renegotiation, or termination. Such a
contract for a lifetime commitment, vague by American standards, does not deal with definite obligations on either side.
However, it is important to realize that there is an implicit
assumption of mutual commitment and goodwill. It is another
example of how the Japanese depend not on legal documents
but on a feeling of shared responsibility, trust, and commitment.

In time the company becomes a home for the new employee, and he is assigned to a more senior member of the
firm who will act as his mentor. This relationship is extremely
important in business life. The "incoming class" of new employees will spend up to six months in orientation and then be
dispersed to different departments, but their first identification will always be with their entering group. Training for new
recruits often includes physical conditioning as well as classes
in company philosophy, human relations, and, of course,
some technical training related to the company. For the first

six to eight years they will all receive the same salary. Thereafter, individual performance and competence will be subtly
rewarded with modest pay raises. During these years they
will work with each other, strengthening the bonds of loyalty
that started with their entry into the company. After about
fifteen years they will be competing for the top jobs. At this
point, management will select those who show the necessary
leadership qualities.

The Japanese usually arrive at work on or before the appointed hour. Often the company reinforces group identity
by holding daily pep talks, by having a group recitation of the
company's creed, or by singing the company song. This gathering is followed by physical exercises. Everyone, from top
management to factory workers, participates in these group
activities. Breaks are rare, though lunch hour is scheduled.
The boss decides when the workday ends; when he leaves,
everyone else in the office can leave, too. It is not so much a
matter of staying late to finish a task as of being on hand
should the boss need an employee. After-hours socializing,
while not technically part of the job, is in reality a recognized
and essential part of it, designed as it is to strengthen bonds
between employees.

The company also provides recreational and vacation facilities to its workers, and some workers live in company-
subsidized housing that may include programs not unlike
those of American summer camps, with early morning runs
and team sports. Competitions are between groups and do
not stress individual achievement. Company sports teams are
very popular, and it's not uncommon to find top management playing on the team with junior managers and factory
workers. Eventually, for many employees, the company becomes the most important thing in their lives. In the words of
Frank Gibney, the Japanese "made the company a village."
The company is also a kind of extended family. The Japanese
often describe someone by saying, "He's a Honda man," or

"He's a Fuji man." Within each company there is a feeling of "we" (uchi, meaning "inside") vs. "they" (soto, or "outside"), "they" being everyone who is not one of "us." Since most employees' social relationships and activities take place within the company framework, the "we/they" dichotomy is reinforced.

There is also a direct relationship between an employee's status and that of his company. Employees depend on their company affiliation in such vital personal matters as marriage (company status is very important to a prospective bride and her family), getting a loan for a house, or even renting an apartment. This dependency on the company reinforces the employee's feeling that his company is his family—another example of the importance of *amae.*

For a revealing account of the day-to-day workings of a typical Japanese company, the reader is referred to a lively article by Jeffrey S. Irish (see Reading List) in which Mr. Irish details his two years as one of the team in a Japanese company.

JAPANESE WORKERS: THE ULTIMATE TEAM PLAYERS

"The Japanese don't want people who do a good job but have a bad attitude."

Japanese CEO, automobile industry

◄◄►►

Most Japanese are hard workers and high achievers, and these qualities are reinforced by intense peer pressure from their *ka* (work group). Above all else, they do not want to let their group down. This feeling of interdependence often makes it very difficult for them to take vacations or sick leave, even when they are very ill, since they feel that absence means failing one's co-workers. Japanese working overseas are often shocked by long vacations and a strict nine-to-five schedule. The difference in work habits is shown in these figures from *The Wall Street Journal* (April 6, 1984): the average German worker clocks 1,773 hours per year, compared to the American's 1,904 and the Japanese worker's 2,101. According to a survey by the Japanese Ministry of Labor in 1983, 30 percent of Japanese salaried workers spend less than three waking hours per day with their families on weekdays; only 41 percent have dinner with their families every day. Despite a determined effort by the government to promote leisure activities, most Japanese continue to work on Saturdays and take only 60 percent of their allotted vacation time each year (see Bernard Wysocki, "Lust for Labor," in Reading List).

Americans must understand the power of the Japanese work ethic if they are to compete with the Japanese. The Japanese man is married first to his job, and then to his family.

LOYALTY

". . . strict adherence to personal loyalty is at the core of Japanese concern for people rather than for principles."

Mark Zimmerman, *How to Do Business with the Japanese*

◄ ◄► ►

Japanese culture is highly situational in character. It has different ethics and moral standards from Western cultures. What Westerners term honesty is overridden by the Japanese desire to protect the boss or the company and to save face at all costs. Even legal contracts and agreements in Japan may change if the situation changes. Since some standards are so fluid, therefore, there must be some constant values on which the Japanese can depend. Loyalty is one of these basic values, remaining constant despite changing circumstances.

When someone commits a crime, those around him feel both great shame and a desire to be protective. For example, when the Japanese Prime Minister, Mr. Tanaka, was accused several years ago of taking bribes from Lockheed, his chauffeur committed suicide rather than risk being called to give testimony in court that might have been damaging to his boss.

The Japanese must demonstrate his loyalty to his group and to his company, most often by staying late and by not taking vacations or sick leave. The Japanese with whom we talked stated, with some embarrassment, that they would prefer to be home with their families, but they felt unable to leave the office as long as the boss was still there. Most said they did not want to let their colleagues down. One German firm in Japan capitalized on the Japanese reluctance to take vacations by arranging company trips to Germany and France, which permitted their employees and those from their franchised businesses to have a vacation with a clear conscience; while they were enjoying themselves, they could make friends with the Europeans with whom they were doing business.

RESPONSIBILITY

Building a reputation for dependability, taking responsibility when something goes wrong, and keeping one's word are all sacred to the Japanese. These characteristics are like "money in the bank." Reliability and dedication are taken for granted. Acknowledging responsibility includes making a public statement that one is truly sorry when a mistake has been made. Contrition is not only valued but is an absolute necessity under certain conditions. Japanese can be very forgiving but not in the absence of contrition.

In Japan, when something goes wrong, the person in charge takes the blame. The form that this takes can range from a straightforward acknowledgment of responsibility to resigning or to *seppuku* (suicide).

One Japanese banker said: "In the United States, decision-making is centralized and responsibility is diffused. In Japan, decision-making is diffused and responsibility is concentrated."

Those reared in cultures stressing individualism are often surprised at the degree of competitiveness that individual Japanese may show in their group-oriented culture. Even when alone, the Japanese knows he has his group behind him, and this group support seems to propel him forward with unbelievable energy. One of the highest goals in life is to be able to contribute to the group against the competition.

QUALITY CONTROL CIRCLES

An American, W. Edward Demming, introduced the concept of quality control in Japanese manufacturing. The Japanese seized upon this idea with alacrity and have developed it far beyond anything that exists in the United States.

Within each large Japanese company there are quality control circles (QCCs) composed of fifteen people from different levels and various departments. They meet regularly to study problems and make recommendations for improvements in products or service. These quality control circles are designed to encourage input from individual employees on ways to improve company performance and to strengthen employee identification with the company. The QCCs compete with each other to discover the best way to save money and reduce waste and defective products. Often the company presents an annual award to its most successful quality control circle. Since significant money-saving suggestions and innovations have come from QCCs, these play an important role in improving overall performance. The goal of quality control is zero defects. QCCs are the modern-day manifestation of the deeply ingrained respect for quality that has been a tradition throughout Japanese history.

For a very brief period before and immediately following World War II, when the Japanese were just beginning to mass-produce goods for the American market, they made cheap toys and small goods of inferior quality. However, they learned about quality control from Demming and then found a great demand for high-quality goods, which is what they've been producing ever since with great success. Since 1951, top Japanese firms have competed for the annual Demming Prize, awarded for outstanding achievement in both productivity and quality control. This is the most sought-after prize in Japanese business today.

SERVICE ORIENTATION

"In Germany your product is most important to your success; in Japan, it is the human relationships you build. Without them you will not succeed."

Manager, trading company

◄◄►►

Japanese business is strongly oriented toward providing service to its customers and is concerned about meeting their needs. Great attention is paid to research on what customers want. One of the frequent complaints about foreign business is that certain firms don't take the trouble to find out what their Japanese customers want. They ship clothing that doesn't fit the Japanese physique and appliances that are too large for Japanese living space and not adapted to lower voltage and frequencies.

The Japanese expect prompt service and availability of a full line of parts for any major purchase. American businesses in Japan must therefore carry a large and complete inventory of parts and provide trained service personnel. This is especially important in the automobile industry since many Japanese fear that buying a foreign car means they won't be able to get parts or good service. (Addressing this fear may be something to consider in your advertising.)

Building customer loyalty is a major goal for Japanese salesmen, and they go to enormous trouble and great effort to give their customers fine service.

THE ORGANIZATION

THE STRUCTURE

 For a comparison between an American and a Japanese business, we refer readers to David Halberstam's *The Reckoning*, which describes Ford and Nissan in great detail.

The organizational structure of Japanese business reflects the hierarchical nature of the society. The division manager, *honbucho*, is above the general manager or division chief, *bucho*, who is above the deputy general manager, *jicho*, who supervises the managers or the department chief, *kacho*. All communication from the top follows the proper chain of command down to the designated employee. If an American executive wants to communicate with one of his *kacho,* he *must* go through the *honbucho, bucho,* and *jicho.* The Japanese do not "jump channels"; this would cause a loss of face for intermediaries.

When an American company works with a Japanese company, it is important that the Americans begin the process of collaboration with those Japanese employees who will be involved. Even if Americans have contacts with top-level people in the Japanese company, they should work only with those Japanese who are working at a comparable level in the Japanese company. After a time, a report on the collaboration will work its way through the information network of the Japanese company to the top-level executives, who will be informed of what has been achieved.

The *ka* is the basic work group of the company and is usually composed of fifteen workers of various ranks and skills plus a *kacho,* or chief. For most workers, the *ka* is the most important group in life next to family and friends. Each worker is assigned to a *ka* for training in more than one task, which makes for flexibility within the organization. Each work group is responsible for a particular job, which means that no one person is ever at fault if a project doesn't succeed. It also means that praise and rewards go not to individuals but only to the group.

Consensus and teamwork are reinforced by many group meetings and prolonged discussion about how to achieve goals. It is management's responsibility to set goals and motivate people to achieve them.

Every three to five years a worker is assigned to a different group, and he will work under several *kacho* before he retires. Most *kacho* have at least fifteen years' experience. Each *kacho* evaluates the worker, suggests what jobs he would do well, and recommends him for other positions.

THE INFORMATION-BASED ORGANIZATION

This movement of personnel within the company reinforces an essential aspect of Japanese organizations: the free flow of information. In every aspect of their lives the Japanese live in a sea of information. On the job, the average American needs procedures and explicit directions; the Japanese does not because he automatically keeps himself constantly informed. He actively participates in sharing all kinds of information, all the time. Usually he works in an area with several other employees, without the screening of a private office; he also talks to other employees and keeps up to date. He listens and watches and learns.

Because the Japanese are high-context, they expect other people to be similarly contexted, that is, informed about everything including office procedures. Their greatest needs are for information about human relationships and how people are feeling. They therefore have quite sensitive antennae for perceiving emotional reactions.

The Japanese mode of sharing information will have an impact on American business. Peter Drucker, writing in *The Wall Street Journal* (June 4, 1985), had this to say about the future of American business:

> " 'The organization of the future' is rapidly becoming reality—a structure in which *information serves as the axis and the central structural support. . . .* Companies are busily reshaping their managerial structure around the flow of information. . . . *It is information rather than authority that enables them to mutually support each other. . . .* The information-based organization requires high self-discipline." [Italics added.]

Much of what Drucker has to say about the information-based organization could have been modeled on a study of Japanese organizations, which are, in the truest sense, information-based. We are convinced that a transition from the traditional Euro-American command-authority organization to the information-based organization alters everything, and there is much to be learned in the process of doing business with the Japanese, whose power lies in their ability to mobilize and use information at all levels.

PROMOTIONS

Before describing the system for promotion, we must emphasize one of the great differences between Japanese and American industry: the quality of the work force. In our opinion, not enough attention is paid to this difference. By and large, Japanese labor is well educated; high school graduates can read, write, and do basic math accurately. Therefore, they can follow instructions and be trained on the job in a very short time. Also, we heard nothing in our interviews about drug or alcohol abuse on the job, a problem that plagues many American industries. In addition, workers are dedicated to their companies and take pride in their products and service.

Routine promotion is automatic by seniority and is not linked to achievement or responsibility. It is given in recognition of the worker's loyalty to the company. This does not mean that talent is lost. It is not. Very talented people are placed where they can best serve the company. When someone is promoted, one of the first things he is asked to do is to choose his successor and begin training him immediately. To be eligible for consideration for promotion, an individual must occupy a position immediately below the position to be filled. No one jumps a rank. He must also have spent the requisite number of years in his previous position.

Most large Japanese companies have ongoing training for their key personnel—those individuals who have been identified as potential leaders. Company personnel departments have extensive information on all employees, their strengths, their special skills, and their weaknesses. They are carefully prepared and given assignments in different parts of the organization, sometimes in different foreign countries as well as at different levels within the company. This insures that they develop the overview considered essential for top management. One Japanese official in a large bank reviewed his company experience for us in such diverse industries as agriculture, manufacturing, and banking. He had had six different foreign assignments. His next project was to be in China, a country of growing interest to Japanese business. Compare his experience with the American practice of developing specialists who remain in one area and work their way up within one division of the company.

The goal of the promotion-selection process is to promote the best man from each age group into the ranks of leadership. The criterion used in judging personnel is performance based on persistence and dependability. Seriousness is highly valued and is demonstrated by hard work, loyalty, and courtesy over a long time. Also needed is the ability to work well in groups. The key to everything in Japan is *ningen kankei*, human relations.

Incompetent workers are few and far between. They are usually "sidelined," given work of minimal importance. Older workers who can no longer be counted on to be productive are permitted to work at routine tasks which allow for "looking out the window," as it was described to us.

LEADERSHIP

"Japanese are like a school of fish; they flow. You don't try to lead them, you just give a slight indication of where they might go, an invisible direction."

Japanese company president, Tokyo

◄ ‹› ►

A term that is very important in understanding the Japanese is *wa,* "harmony." It refers to the quality of human relationships and involves cooperation, trust, sharing, and warmth, based on a caring attitude toward others. It is the ingredient that results in efficient teamwork and high morale. The success of any enterprise, small or large, depends on harmony, beginning with the smallest unit and going up through all levels of the organization. The successful leader does his best to contribute to and enhance *wa.*

Top Japanese executives are chosen for their leadership qualities. As they rise through the ranks, employees are carefully watched and rated on their own performance, particularly their ability to get along with others and work harmoniously with their team. To the Japanese, *leadership means an individual's ability to listen carefully to others and to work to achieve group consensus and harmony.* These are the marks of a leader. Judgment and the ability to combine a long-term view with a wide-ranging perspective are also important. A good Japanese executive is like an old-time sea captain. He knows his ship, he knows his men, and he knows the sea. He never touches the helm and he never endangers his ship; he depends on his officers and his crew and he keeps an eye on everything.

Japanese leadership positions require seniority within the organization and the strong support of one's personal associates, who are loyal and devoted to their leader. In the rare instance when a new leader is brought in from another part of the organization or from outside, he brings with him his own group *(kobun)*, who are personally loyal to him and both dependent on and supportive of him. The golden rule of Japanese ethics is, "No man can serve two masters."

Nowhere is the contrast between Japanese and American culture more pronounced than in their different concepts of leadership. In the United States, a leader is usually someone with a strong ego, often with personal charisma, selected for his ability to make decisions and to take responsibility with or without consulting his associates. This kind of "take charge" leader who wants to "put his stamp" on the organization can be devastating to the Japanese because he destroys the sense of harmony and consensus that is vital to their performance.

The title of Thomas Rohlen's book, *For Harmony and Strength,* is taken from a bank motto. Rohlen writes:

> "Those considered top leadership material are generally men with a surplus of energy, intelligence, and ambition, qualities they must learn to control and discipline in order to survive the long years of subordination to the organization, their superiors, and their office groups. For the average man this subordination may not be particularly difficult, but for the talented and vital people it can be a struggle."

As many observers have noted, Japanese learn to develop great inner strength as they grow up and mature. Their self-control enables them to master any hostile or antisocial feelings that might be disruptive to the group.

HIERARCHY: BUSINESS CARDS AND BOWS

The Japanese are very hierarchical and have systems for ranking everyone and everything; therefore, the first thing a Japanese wants to know about any outsider is where that individual is located in his company. Japanese cannot relate properly to someone without this information. This is why business calling cards *(meishi)* are important in Japan. They are used on every occasion when one businessman meets another. The cards should be engraved or printed on fine quality paper. Foreign executives must have calling cards with their name, company name and address, and, most important, their title, indicating their rank in the company. For foreigners, it is customary to have one side of the card printed in English and the other side in Japanese characters to make it possible for the Japanese to place you correctly. Until a Japanese knows your position (rank) in your company he does not know how to relate to you, how deferential to be. He cannot establish a relationship with you until he has this information.

The Japanese businessman who receives two or more cards at the same meeting will usually place them on a table in front of him and position them according to rank. Cards are especially helpful in a group meeting. It is best to carry cards in a card case in your jacket. There is a ritual for exchanging calling cards and it must be followed exactly. First, make sure the card is not presented to the Japanese upside down. As in all matters of Japanese courtesy, it is wise to have some coaching. When you receive a business card, read what's on it and always take it with you. It is customary to present one card at a time to each member of a group, with the proper formal bow. We once witnessed an example of how it should not be done when a European businessman threw his calling cards on the table as if he were dealing cards in a poker game.

It was highly embarrassing to all present, especially his Japanese boss.

There are many subtle signs of rank in Japan which may not be apparent to American visitors. As mentioned earlier, the Japanese language constantly conveys superior or subordinate rank. Another more obvious manifestation is the manner in which they bow. The Japanese bow at the beginning of each meeting or interaction and again at the end. It is possible to sit in a hotel lobby in Japan and determine the relative rank of Japanese by the manner in which they bow to each other. The person with the least status bows lowest.

Hierarchy is so ingrained in Japanese society that the Japanese do not need status symbols such as private offices or executive dining rooms to convey rank; however, the position of the desk or the chair in a large room is all-important. In general, the chair farthest from the door is the place of honor. Top Japanese executives sometimes eat in the company cafeteria and wear the company work jackets in their offices. This signifies their identification with the company team, but it does not mean that anyone is unaware of their rank. This sensitivity to rank extends to wives of Japanese executives, who are careful to defer to the boss's wife and are very solicitous and helpful to her. Subordinate wives do not appear with clothes or jewelry that might be considered more elegant than those of the boss's wife; this would cause her to lose face.

COLLECTIVE DECISION-MAKING AND CONSENSUS: THE "RINGI"—SLOW, SLOW; FAST, FAST

By now, most foreign business executives have heard about the importance of consensus in Japanese business—indeed, in every facet of Japanese life. Harmony and consensus are keystones of Japanese society. In business, any new project is presented in a proposal called the *ringi*, giving the goal, the expected benefits of achieving it, the pros and cons, the cost, and the projected time frame. The *ringi* slowly works its way through many layers of the organization, with frequent delays for changes and clarification. This process of collective decision-making allows everyone involved a chance to review, evaluate, discuss, and approve or disapprove the proposal. This process is absolutely essential in a society where individuals need to be fully informed about everything. When an individual approves a proposal, he puts his personal stamp *(han)* on it; some proposals have dozens of stamps before the process is completed. The finished document with everyone's stamp is called the *ringisho*. Until the *ringisho* is completed, there is no final decision.

Final decisions entail many, many meetings, where all points of view are presented and discussed until consensus is achieved. At every stage differences are reconciled. The *ringi* system not only insures that each employee is fully informed and consulted, but it insures strong support for the final decision. This kind of "bottom-up" decision-making means many ideas are initiated from middle and lower levels in the company. If management wants to take the initiative with a proposal, it assigns a staff member the job of preparing the proposal; like all other proposals, it will work its way through all levels of the *ringi* process.

Japanese decision-making causes Americans great distress because they don't understand the delays. They consider it "foot dragging," which it is not. However, the short implementation time may compensate for the delay in decision-making. Because everyone identifies closely with the final decision, each employee works hard to implement it, hence the description, "slow, slow; fast, fast." It's also important to remember that in a system of lifetime employment in one of the major firms, decisions that affect the future of the company have great personal impact on each employee; he knows he will have to live with the results of these decisions. Everyone wants to be sure they are realistic and beneficial, both for him and for his company.

It is important to know that while 90 percent of decision making in Japanese business is consensus, there are a few exceptions. In companies where the CEO is also the founder of the company, he may sometimes make a unilateral decision, which is called *tsuru no hitoke,* "one screech of the crane." *Tsuru no hitoke* is so unusual that when it occurs the CEO may feel obligated to explain or justify his decision to his subordinates.

Because of consensus decision-making, Japanese board meetings are a ritual. The president reads the minutes and everyone present says, "No objection" to each point. There is no discussion because decisions are being reported, not made. Exhaustive discussions have already been held before the meeting at every level in the organization. The board meeting is therefore a formal ceremony acknowledging what has been decided.

LONG-TERM PLANNING

Long-term planning is a cornerstone of Japanese business. Companies take planning for granted, and it is built into their day-to-day operations. Examples of long-term planning in Japan abound. For instance, many companies now know who their managers will be in the year 2000; other companies are already deeply involved in future projects such as the Osaka Festival for the 21st Century (this festival, still fourteen years in the future, now has an office for coordinating the project).

Top management is committed to investing profits in research and development for the future, since they are much less concerned with immediate profits and with stockholders than with long-term financial health. Japanese companies also accumulate capital to modernize plants and develop new technologies. This is part of their future planning, as is their practice of investing in personnel training. Companies in the United States that are unable to think of the long term are under a severe handicap when competing with the Japanese.

STRIKES

The well-known spring labor offensive in Japan, called the *shunto,* is the time of year when unions publicize their demands and workers march with loudspeakers blaring. During this time there is usually a threat of a strike by the national railway workers' union. For the most part it is only unions of government workers that actually go on strike. Private unions usually take a more cooperative position with company management.

The Japanese do not have trade unions. Each large company has its own union, which represents all employees except top executives. As a result, the union concentrates on working conditions in the company rather than on those throughout the industry. Company strikes are very infrequent, but they pose a much greater danger to the company than industry-wide strikes. Workers are aware of the vulnerability of their company during a strike because they know competitors might take advantage of the chance to injure the company permanently.

The union monitors the company's overall performance and works to resolve differences between union and management. Since many directors of major Japanese companies once served as company labor leaders in their younger years, management is sensitive to labor's concerns. Another important factor in understanding the position of labor is the re-

quired disclosure of financial data. All public companies in
Japan are required to publish profit-and-loss balance sheets in
the newspapers. Financial data are well known, both inside
and outside the company. As one German managing director
of a large manufacturing company in Japan told us, "This is a
company with glass pockets. Everyone knows our financial
situation." Personal financial information is also widely available—a list of everyone who earns more than 10 million yen
a year (approximately $40,000 in 1985) is published annu-
ally. Unions know their company's financial position; they
know workers will share in profits through bonuses during
good years, and that they must also share bad times when
bonuses may be reduced or omitted. For example, in 1986
several large Japanese manufacturers reduced pay for their
senior executives by 10 percent because profits were down.
The free flow of information, in this instance between labor
and management, is a great factor in successful collaboration
and internal harmony.

The salary ratio between labor and top management for
three industrialized countries is given below:

United States	1	to	80
West Germany	1	to	25
Japan	1	to	7

It's easy to understand why the Japanese worker feels he's
part of the team.

It would be a fallacy to think that all Japanese workers are
well protected, since there is lifetime employment only for
employees of the large, major companies, which make up
only 30 percent of companies nationwide. The mandatory
retirement age is 55–57, except for directors and senior executives. Retirement is a painful time for Japanese workers because they do not usually have company pensions. Instead,
workers merely receive a lump-sum payment at retirement.
(Some Japanese workers have government pensions to which

they have contributed, but these are very modest.) For most Japanese, retirement simply means the age at which a man must leave his company and try to find another job. Sometimes companies agree to keep a retired worker at a reduced wage. In 1980, half the Japanese men over sixty-five were still working and many others were looking for jobs. Retirement is a period of financial strain on the retiree, and often his children have to contribute to his support. The situation poses severe problems for the Japanese in the future, as the aged are becoming a larger and larger proportion of the population.

WOMEN IN BUSINESS

"Resignation is the first lesson of life."

Yomiko Yansson

Japanese business has traditionally been a man's world. There are very few women in business, and those are usually found only in clerical or secretarial jobs. The large corporations usually do not hire women except as secretaries on a temporary basis. Women are viewed as "temporary employees" who will leave their jobs when they marry. Even women who have graduated from Tokyo University and other prestigious universities have great difficulty finding appropriate jobs. In a New York *Times* article on women in business, Susan Chira reported that, according to the Japanese Ministry of Labor, women accounted for about 35 percent of the salaried work force in Japan in 1983, yet only 6 percent of its managers. Female managers were less than one tenth of 1 percent of all working women in the country.

The situation is gradually changing. Recently, American business and a few major Japanese firms have begun hiring

Japanese female university graduates, taking advantage of their training, ability, and intelligence. We predict this trend will continue, since these women are a great untapped resource.

According to a 1981 Japanese government survey, women represent 43 percent of the 350,000 Japanese who work for foreign firms. Since many Japanese men do not want to work for foreign firms, American business is discovering how advantageous it is to hire well-educated Japanese women. Some of them now hold top executive posts in such American industries as banking, publishing, and consumer products.

THE FUTURE

Conditions are changing, and no one knows how long the tradition of loyalty and the strong Japanese work ethic will remain intact. The impetus for change comes from economic factors and from contact with the Americans, Germans, and other Europeans, who think little of changing jobs. In these countries, workers' careers are their own and are not tied to the company. As a matter of fact, in many Western countries, the only way middle or top management can advance is by changing jobs, a pattern that radically alters feelings of loyalty to a company. A company with little employee turnover, where the career of the employees is allied with the future of the company, is a very different organization from one in which the company is seen as a means for personal advancement.

Japan's rising standard of living is also bringing about many changes. For example, the work week in 1985 was 40.5 hours, compared to 47.6 in 1960. Younger workers in particular are less willing to work overtime, and more and more Japanese of all ages are taking longer vacations. It would appear that the Japanese are becoming more interested in leisure and in enjoying life. This is not to say that there are no longer workers and managers who continue to put in twelve-hour days. But there is a strong current pushing the Japanese toward a less obsessive work orientation. Many Japanese workers and management now want more promotions based on performance. Young Japanese want more time for their families. Japanese women are trying hard to get a foothold in business and are no longer willing to be only temporary employees. It's impossible to predict how quickly such changes will become widely accepted.

Traditionally the Japanese have been great savers. In 1985 they saved on average 17 percent of their disposable income. In a recent effort to stimulate consumer spending and thus encourage sales of imported goods, the government is reducing or abolishing savings incentives. The government is also contemplating tax cuts to spur housing construction and large-scale public works projects.

WHY JAPANESE BUSINESS IS SUCCESSFUL

"Japan isn't just a formidable economic challenge, it is a devastating mental challenge."

American executive, electronics industry

"Tremendous dedication, hard work and unstinting personal sacrifice and effort were the secret of Japan's postwar economic recovery; they remain to a considerable extent the secret of Japan's rousing success in the competition among the advanced industrial nations for a share of the world's market. . . ."

Roy Andrew Miller, *Japan's Modern Myth*

◄ ◄ ► ►

We are frequently asked why Japanese business is so successful. Is it just because employees work harder? Certainly this is one important factor, but there are many others. Japanese business has learned to work effectively with employees who are well educated and who already have a strong, built-in work ethic. Japanese business stresses teamwork and rewards team efforts, not individual efforts. Quality control is promoted at every level, and, most important, there is a steady flow of information throughout the organization. Everyone has access to vital information about his job and about the company's performance. The company creed is taken seriously and employees feel a duty to serve the public well. When the company does well, everyone shares in the rewards. Most employees stay long enough to see their long-term plans come to fruition. All these factors build strong identification with the company and a strong corporate culture.

Of course, Japanese business has its problems, many of which are a reflection of problems in the society. Extreme conformity numbs creativity. Not every Japanese can be a team player and not everyone performs well in groups. For the individualist, life in Japan is difficult. The Japanese have a saying, "The nail that sticks up gets pounded down." Undoubtedly, the talent and creativity of many Japanese has been stifled or lost.

For Americans it is important to remember that despite their great prosperity the Japanese continue to feel very vulnerable. The "oil shock" of the 1970s rocked the country and brought home to Japanese how dependent they are on imports of strategic materials. This vulnerability fuels their competitive drive. They are determined to be Number One. The company's rank is more important than profit to Japanese business, and each employee feels that his company's prestige affects his social and financial status. All these systems, economic and social, reinforce each other. Is it any wonder Japan is such a formidable competitor?

"JAPAN, INC."

The Japanese Ministry of International Trade and Industry, known as MITI, works closely with major Japanese corporations. (See Chalmers Johnson's book, *MITI and the Japanese Miracle.)* MITI encourages cooperation between government and business, industry and technology. This close collaboration is sometimes referred to as "Japan, Inc." MITI works with Japanese business as a friend and advisor. We heard many complaints from foreign business executives, American and European alike, about the protectionist policies of MITI. Whether or not this is a major cause of difficulties facing foreign business, the perception of foreign business is that the Japanese government protects Japanese industry from foreign competition by its regulations. Despite recent liberalization, there are still some restrictions on imports and many required inspections and procedures for all foreign goods. We were told about stalling tactics in issuing import permits which resulted in long delays in getting merchandise to the Japan market. Sometimes goods have to sit on the docks for months. Obviously, such delays pose real problems for foreign business. While these complaints may well be valid, many observers feel that cultural barriers play a far greater role than trade barriers.

Possibly one reason for the close cooperation between Japanese business and MITI is the fact that government ministries are highly regarded by the Japanese. Some graduates of the best Japanese universities enter government service, which has great prestige and authority. It's comparable to the situation in France, where graduates of the top schools, *"les grandes écoles,"* enter the ranks of French ministries. Ministry officials in both countries have great status and are charged with being the guardians of the national interest. MITI cooperates closely with business because business fuels Japan's economy. It's a far cry from the adversarial relations that American business has with U.S. government agencies. More than one American business executive observed that he wished the American government would be as helpful and supportive to business as MITI. Several American executives criticized American government bureaucracies for their delays in allowing goods to be shipped to Japan. (There are presently fifteen U.S. agencies that handle trade decisions.) As one American manager said, "American bureaucrats are worse than the Japanese. Sometimes it's just impossible to get any action."

Japanese business is regulated by strict, highly technical, and demanding laws and procedures; however, these regulations are not normally applied to everyday situations as they are in the United States. Instead, regulations are consciously held in reserve as powerful social safeguards and are only applied when the situation seems to warrant it. Like a powerful but benign parent, the Japanese government prefers to allow leeway so that people and institutions who get into trouble have the chance to work their way out. We interviewed foreign managers of Japanese firms who commented on the unbelievable amount of scope they were given in running their businesses. This freedom stems from the Japanese belief that they must give everyone a chance to succeed. They realize that it is not efficient to keep either people or businesses in a tightly circumscribed legal box.

There are all sorts of informal messages ("administrative guidance") sent by the Japanese government when it doesn't think a business is doing something correctly, but the foreigner may not know how to read the signs. We were told

that if things should go so far that the law must be applied due
to some violation, then something is seriously wrong and
should have been corrected earlier. Somebody failed to read
the warning signs and let matters slide too long. The future
outlook in such a case would not be promising. Rules governing leeway in the application of government regulations
are *unwritten*. The best advice is to have a Japanese on your
staff who is competent to advise on matters of this sort.

The difference between the two systems is that in the
United States business firms don't take any action until the
federal agencies notify them that the company is in violation
of regulations. In Japan, when you get an official notice of a
violation, it is frequently too late to do anything.

THE BANKS AND THE COMPANY

Japanese business firms are closely tied to their bankers
because most companies finance their operations with
money from their banks. Japanese bankers are often deeply
involved with their business clients, sometimes even in day-
to-day operations. It is not unusual to find bankers on the
boards of Japanese companies. Since Japanese business depends on bank financing to a greater degree than American
business, it's only natural that the bankers keep close watch
on their business and their clients. Stockholders are not a
significant factor in financing most Japanese businesses.

Banks provide a great variety of services for their clients,
far beyond what is provided by American banks (see Zimmerman, Chapter 12). Your Japanese bankers can be an invaluable asset.

BUSINESS, LARGE AND SMALL

Japanese business is divided into two main categories. First are the major corporations that work closely with the Ministry of International Trade and Industry (MITI). These large Japanese corporations employ approximately one third of the Japanese work force. Usually, they hire only at the entry level and offer lifetime employment and generous employee benefits. Approximately 30 percent of Japanese firms are in this category. You will probably be dealing with some of them.

The second category, comprising 70 percent of Japanese firms, is that of smaller businesses employing the other two thirds of the work force. Smaller companies often have ties to the large companies and do subcontracting work. Companies in the second category do *not* offer lifetime employment, and, naturally, there are great differences between the two in pay, working conditions, and prestige. For the major companies, the advantage of subcontracting is that in times of recession they can reduce their orders to subcontractors and avoid having to fire their own employees. However, this system means that life is more precarious for smaller companies and their employees.

THE JAPANESE MARKET

Japan is a small country, about the size of California, and only 20 percent of it is arable and habitable. It has virtually no physical resources, yet it supports over 120 million people. It is the largest industrial and consumer market in Asia and the second largest market in the world.

In 1984 the Japanese gross national product (GNP) was $1.1 trillion (U.S.), and its 1984 trade surplus was $44 billion.

Japan's GNP is the second largest in the world, and by the year 2000 it is expected to surpass that of the United States, which is currently the leader. In trade with the United States, Japan had a $50 billion surplus in 1985. According to *Time* (April 16, 1985), the top U.S. exports to Japan in descending order were corn, chemicals, soybeans, office machines, aircraft and parts, coal, and lumber. Only three are manufactured products. For automobiles the Japanese market is the second largest in the world, yet foreign imports account for only 1.4 percent of this market. As one American executive in Tokyo expressed it, "Our problem is our products don't meet Japanese standards. The quality is not dependable and the service is poor."

Japanese consumers follow the latest trends, thus creating a market that changes quickly and can be unstable. Japanese manufacturers often work with very low profit margins, which adds to the instability of the market. The success of a company in Japan may well depend on its ability to adapt its product to Japanese needs and produce it at a lower cost than the competition. This means there isn't much cushion for the producer if the company misjudges the popularity of a product. However, in the words of a successful American businessman in Tokyo:

> "You *can* do business in Japan. Don't be discouraged by other Americans who tell you how difficult it is. They just don't want any more competition."

As Robert Christopher states in *Second to None,* there are ample opportunities for American industry to increase its market share in Japan. We will deal with these opportunities in the next section, "The American Company in Japan."

Part IV 吉

THE AMERICAN COMPANY IN JAPAN

STARTING BUSINESS IN JAPAN

"The real trade barriers are cultural barriers that have nothing to do with quotas or regulations."

American director, consumer products company

SOME COMMON AMERICAN EXPECTATIONS

1. "There will be order in procedures and presentations, with a logical exposition of ideas."—On the contrary, Japanese are people-oriented rather than procedure-oriented. Rigid agendas do not fit the Japanese need for flexibility and information. In fact, the Japanese react negatively to linear Western logic.
2. "Procedures will be followed faithfully."—See above.
3. "Detailed information will be provided about everything."—Wrong. The Japanese are high-context and expect others to be equally well informed. Be prepared for surprises if you have not done all your homework.
4. "Privacy and personal space will be protected from intrusion."—Expect the opposite. There is little concept of privacy in Japan as Westerners know it.
5. "Formality and politeness (including respect for status) pervades day-to-day business life."—Yes, the Japanese are extremely polite and considerate. They treat all

strangers politely, but that does not necessarily mean that they like them.

6. "Frankness and forthrightness should govern human interactions."—Wrong again. Indirection is the basic Japanese approach. One must learn to avoid directness, exactness, and being overly specific.

One American executive expressed his business priorities as follows:

> "The U.S. has become the leading business and financial country because of our honesty in negotiating, our directness, and our desire for swift results."

Of the three, only honesty will favorably impress the Japanese.

THE NEED FOR A LONG-TERM PLAN

> "Don't go to Japan unless you're ready to make a long-term commitment in both time and money. It takes many, many years."
>
> Tokyo banker

◄◄►►

Any American company that expects to do business in Japan needs a long-term plan. This means starting at least *five years in advance.* Like all high-context people, the Japanese need to develop personal relationships with their business associates, and establishing these relationships takes time. The Japanese do not like strangers who come and go. Among foreign companies in Japan, there is a very high correlation between length of time in Japan and success. Unfortunately, many American businesses don't understand this and give up too soon.

We were told that in the preliminary stages of assessing the Japanese market, companies should begin a simultaneous two-pronged program, one in the United States and one in Japan.

INITIAL PROGRAM IN THE U.S.

1. Consult your bankers for their advice and assistance. Some American banks have branches in Japan; others can put you in touch with American bank personnel in Japan as well as with their contacts in Japanese banks, all of whom are in a position to advise you about many aspects of doing business in Japan.

2. Consult Japanese banks in the United States for advice and assistance. Your goal is to develop some contacts in Japan who can guide you and introduce you both to the bankers who will be helpful and to American executives in Japan who may be willing to offer assistance.

3. Consult the Japanese External Trade Organization (JETRO) offices in the United States. Major cities such as Los Angeles and New York have these offices and can refer you to others. JETRO is a storehouse of information about business in Japan. Its English-language publications cover the basics of what American business needs to know to begin to understand the complexity of Japanese business. JETRO also has a number of very fine films concerning cultural differences.

4. Talk to the Japanese consuls in your area.

The purpose of these initial contacts in the United States is to begin to build a network of contacts in Japan, the so-called "magic circle" that will be essential to everything you do later. You will also learn a great deal from talking to bankers and JETRO personnel, as well as the Japanese consul. Remember, the Japanese have a wealth of information to share, but they must first get to know you.

INITIAL VISIT TO JAPAN: KEEP IT SIMPLE

Choosing the right individual to make the initial investigation in Japan is important. This mission should not be delegated to a subordinate but given to a top executive who will be involved with the Japanese operation, either in the home office or in Japan. This person should be experienced, intelligent, flexible, and interested in other countries.

The whole trip should take a minimum of two weeks; anything less is simply not enough time. Armed with background information, the investigator should go with two purposes in mind: to identify a niche in the market, if there is one, and to assess the size of that market potential to see if it is large enough to warrant the expense of a more detailed feasibility study. He should avoid activating a lot of people. It is much better, much simpler for him, if no one knows he is there. Having studied some of the best books on the Japanese and Japanese business, he will know where to look, and he should be able to do this freely, without distractions, so that he can make up his own mind. While he's spending time in Tokyo he should watch television to see what products are advertised and how; he should also visit the American Chamber of Commerce and read some of its publications. He should also visit other Japanese cities. We would suggest that at this stage he not contact the Japanese; that comes later.

If, on the basis of the initial visit, your company decides to enter the Japanese market, the first task is the selection of the executive to head your Japanese office. This person should be someone who gets along well with people, is sensitive to cultural differences, has a high language aptitude, and has a strong drive to maintain good interpersonal relations. He must be able to negotiate with the Japanese. A high proportion of the most successful American executives we interviewed were those who had lived abroad; they grew up in a foreign country, had attended schools abroad, or had worked overseas. The overseas experience sensitizes people to cross-cultural differences and makes it much easier to adjust to a culture as different as Japan's. There are today in the United States thousands of men and women who have had extensive overseas experience, either in the Peace Corps or in some other form of government service. There are also many people who have lived abroad with their parents who were in foreign service or international business. This resource deserves careful consideration in recruiting personnel for international assignments.

Thoroughly prepare your top executive in Japan. After recruiting the very best person within the company, make sure he or she is willing to make a *long-term* commitment to Japan. We were told over and over again how important it is for foreign executives to stay in Japan long enough to learn the language and something about the culture. A minimum of five to six years is required before foreigners can begin to grasp the complexity of the Japanese mentality and understand how business works. After ten years, the American executive can begin to comprehend the problems. Some of the most competent people we interviewed had been in Japan twenty years or more. To ensure fluency in the language, the manager must begin studying Japanese every day for at least five years and should continue daily language study for several years thereafter.

Your top manager for Japan, particularly if different from the person who made the initial visit, should go to Japan to begin the groundwork for setting up the Japanese operations. This is the time to initiate serious talks with your Japanese advisors.

CHECKLIST FOR STARTING UP IN JAPAN

1. *Consult the Japan External Trade Organization (JETRO).* JETRO can advise on many aspects of conducting business in Japan, and it also publishes numerous booklets on specialized aspects of business in Japan. Start by studying JETRO's excellent book *Doing Business in Japan,* which outlines some essential procedures.

2. *Consult the commercial attaché at the American embassy in Tokyo and the staff of the American Chamber of Commerce.* The Chamber of Commerce is prepared to offer both helpful advice and reading materials and can refer you to American business executives working in Japan.

3. *Stay in Japan long enough to study the market in depth.* Visit the major cities and manufacturing areas, become familiar with retail outlets, watch television for at least two to three days, both day and evening (paying special attention to Japanese advertising), and gather enough information about the potential demand for your company's product or services to ascertain where they fit in the Japanese market. This requires considerable time and effort, and is very expensive, especially for small businesses. Yet, we were told that small companies are often highly successful. There is no substitute for studying these things firsthand. No report, no statistical tables, can compare with firsthand knowledge of the complexities and diversities of the Japanese market.

4. *Consult with your banking contacts in Japan,* both American and Japanese. They can introduce you to reliable people.

5. *Seek the advice and assistance of an experienced Japanese executive,* preferably one who has recently retired from a top position in a company in your industry. Your

bankers can be helpful in recommending such a person. This retired executive can assist you in many ways, help you start your business, and recruit qualified staff.

6. *Confer with leading management consulting firms.* Your bankers can recommend reliable, experienced firms.

7. *Interview some major trading companies (sogo shosha)* to decide if a trading company is required to establish your Japanese operation. Trading companies handle 68 percent of Japan's imports and 44 percent of its exports. They represent viable alternatives to licensing or setting up a foreign subsidiary and are sometimes preferable because they already know the ropes of the intricate Japanese distribution system.

8. *Consult attorneys* who specialize in registration of trademarks and patents to determine the specific action your company must take to protect itself in Japan. This vital step has been overlooked by some companies, to their detriment.

THE JAPANESE CONNECTION

"The importance of proper *entrée* cannot be overstated. You can have the very finest product made, but you'll never sell it in Japan without the right connections."

Managing director, consumer product company

"You cannot do business in Japan without the right connections to an old, well-respected Japanese company."

Banker in Japan

‹ ‹›› ›

Entrée into the Japanese market—in fact, everything you do in Japan—depends on the quality of your Japanese associates. Your Japanese bankers and advisors can assist you and introduce you to the right people in your industry. Your network becomes your key to success, your magic circle.

Without proper connections to well-respected banks, trading companies, and customs agents, or a partnership with a large and respected Japanese company, it is almost impossible to succeed. Even with the proper Japanese partners it takes longer to start your business and build up market share than it would at home. Most executives told us to *allow at least ten years*. Great patience is required. There will be many meetings, many late nights of after-hours entertaining, dinners followed by evenings at private clubs or "singing bars," weekends of golf and tennis games—all designed to help your representative and your prospective Japanese partners get to know each other.

Joint ventures are one solution for American companies in Japan. Such an association makes it much easier to handle your problems with the Japanese. However, it again depends on the quality of your partner in the venture, and you will need advice and counsel from your bankers and other advisors. Joint ventures are no guarantee of success. One Japanese in the import-export business told us, "When I engaged in a joint venture operation where both Japanese and Americans tried to cook the broth, I became exposed to what you call the Ugly American, and vice versa."

For some case histories of American business firms in Japan, we refer our readers to Robert Christopher's *Second to None*. We also urge you to study some of the best books on Japanese business, beginning with Zimmerman's *How to Do Business with the Japanese;* also highly recommended are

Abegglen's and Stalk's *Kaisha, The Japanese Corporation,*
Gibney's *Japan: The Fragile Super Power* and *Miracle by
Design,* Norbury's and Bownas' *Business in Japan,* Pascale's
and Athos' *The Art of Japanese Management,* Rohlen's *For
Harmony and Strength,* and Taylor's *Shadows of the Rising
Sun.* Other recommended publications are the daily *Japan
Economic Journal* (Nihon Keizai Shimbun, Inc.), *The Wall
Street Journal,* and the business sections of the New York
Times, the Washington *Post,* and the Los Angeles *Times,* and
periodicals such as *Business Week, Forbes,* and *Fortune.*

LEARNING THE LANGUAGE

"Those who don't learn Japanese will find a real
barrier erected between themselves and real understanding of the Japanese. In Japanese it is not
only what is said that is important—how it is said
can be far more important."

Mark Zimmerman, *How to Do Business with the Japanese*

◄ ◄►►

Since language is a direct reflection of culture and thus one
of the keys to understanding the mentality of a people, any
American company involved in the Japanese market will
have an advantage by insisting that its principal employees
speak Japanese. In fact, this was the primary recommendation of the many Japanese business executives we interviewed. Several long-term residents of Japan told us that it is
impossible *not* to stay informed if one speaks the language.
But that "if" is one of the most important factors imaginable.

It is neither possible nor necessary for a foreigner to be
letter-perfect. The Japanese have in recent years become
very sympathetic to the foreigner who makes a reasonable

effort to speak their language, and they do not expect that a foreigner will speak like a Japanese. But if you can't speak the language at all, there will be a question in Japanese minds as to whether you should be doing business in their country.

Remember, the Japanese language relies on very subtle cues and reveals the attitude of the speaker toward his interlocutors, which is a vitally important piece of information.

It is essential to decide what level of fluency one wishes to achieve, because there are no shortcuts to learning Japanese. If you wish to be able to conduct business with Japanese in their language, many years of hard work will be required. According to expert linguists, mastering enough Japanese to be able to conduct business requires a minimum of two years, full time, in school. These years must then be followed by daily study and regular tutorials. Obviously, such a program is difficult and time-consuming, yet many of the most successful and respected businessmen urged its necessity. Also, such intensive study of the language should begin before age thirty, which means that American businesses must plan ahead and begin training their younger executives for future assignments in Japan.

For those executives whose goals are more modest, who want only to be able to speak a few polite phrases and give brief, simple talks, several months of classes or tutoring will be required along with daily practice. We caution Americans not to expect instant results. Be wary of any school that promises miraculous shortcuts. One distinguished American linguist, an expert Japanese-language instructor, was approached by an American company to give a two-day course in Japanese. The company had no idea how ridiculous this request was.

Remember that the Japanese begin studying English in the seventh grade and continue throughout high school and college. Those who will be working in the United States have often studied for twenty or more years. Of course, English is very difficult for the Japanese, but they also understand how important it is to devote time to learning the language.

FRIENDSHIPS: ESSENTIAL RELATIONSHIPS

Personal relationships are very important to the Japanese; indeed, they are crucial in building working relationships, and there are no shortcuts to developing them. Many American executives told us they spend three or four nights a week with their Japanese customers and staff. To do business, you must first get to know each other; since you are playing in their territory, use their rules. There are times when a friend in the right place can mean the difference between success and failure.

Be aware that in Japan personal relationships and friendships tend to take a long time to solidify. Because of the Japanese hierarchical system, which integrates many Japanese into close-knit networks of schoolmates and relatives, it is extraordinarily difficult for a foreigner to break in. Nevertheless, the American executive would do well to develop some close friendships with Japanese.

In the United States, developing friendships is easy enough. In fact, people in this country can become friends in a very short time. As we explained earlier, Americans have a worldwide reputation for being able to form only superficial, informal friendships that lack the exchange of deep confidences. Americans start out immediately trying to be jovial by first-naming and "glad-handing." Such behavior doesn't fool the Japanese for a minute. They may call you by your first name, but this doesn't mean they consider you a friend; they are merely imitating the popular conception of what Americans are like. Since close friendships in Japan, as well as being personally significant, are crucial to business, we caution Americans never to attempt to fake a relationship.

You may find that once you meet a Japanese and it seems likely that you will be seeing each other often, he will begin to tell you things about himself. These revelations function in at least two ways: they context you by giving you background information about the person, and they preserve privacy, since he selects what to tell and what to keep to himself. In the interest of reciprocity, therefore, it may be helpful for the American to reveal somewhat more of himself than he is accustomed to doing.

The Japanese have a conviction that no foreigner (gaijin) can ever really understand them, and in a way they are correct. However, there are many things one can do, and one of the most important is to form a close friendship. You can learn things from friends, who can explain things that casual acquaintances cannot or will not.

ENTERTAINMENT AND GIFTS

Americans are usually overwhelmed by Japanese hospitality and politeness. The Japanese are consummate hosts. They will wine and dine you, be solicitous of your every wish, take care of you from the moment you arrive until you depart. They may have breakfast, lunch, and dinner with you, and take you to favorite bars and cabarets. In fact, Japanese business spends $18 billion a year entertaining clients in restaurants and bars and on the golf course.

In time, more and more of the invisible aspects of Japanese culture will be revealed to you—invisible because the important part of the message is in the context and not in the overt, visible communication. The meal is one example: it expresses the need to relate to each other and to learn as much as possible about everything that affects one's business or organization. The preparation and presentation of a meal is an aesthetic performance, an art form. The colors, textures, aromas, and arrangement or organization of each dish, as well as the order in which dishes are served, are all a part of the composition. Even the personality and status of the guest are taken into account. The meal is a message to the guest as to the importance of the occasion; however, laden as it is with messages about personal status, the meal is not for specific discussions of business. Leave details of work at the office and use the opportunity instead to enjoy yourself and get to know your colleagues as human beings.

One word of caution: do not mistake Japanese hospitality for friendship. The two are not the same thing. Your prospective Japanese partners may overwhelm you with kindness and gifts—that is standard practice. But they know how to "play hardball," too, and they do so when you begin negotiating.

Gifts are especially important in Japan in business and personal relationships. It is customary to bring your Japanese associates gifts from abroad. They particularly appreciate liquor, candy, food, or handicrafts from foreign countries. See JETRO's 1982 pamphlet for examples of appropriate gifts. As a visitor you will receive gifts, and it's important to know that one never refuses a gift. It's the ultimate insult in Japan.

One occasion at which gifts are very important is weddings of employees, business clients, or acquaintances. If you are invited to a wedding reception, there are definite rules about gifts. Japanese etiquette books describe in detail the kind of gift that is expected from people at different levels in the social and economic hierarchy, including the amount that you should expect to spend on gifts for people in different categories. Wedding receptions are a major expense, comparable to a down payment on a house, and often cost as much as fifty thousand dollars for top business executives and their families. Hence the need for guests to reciprocate with appropriate gifts. Seek the advice of your Japanese staff.

ESTABLISHING JAPANESE OPERATIONS

Once your top manager has consulted with trading companies and patent attorneys, he will begin recruiting Japanese personnel. This is a crucial task. The importance of effective recruitment cannot be overstated. Many successful managers made this recommendation: select top-quality professional personnel consultants in Japan and then *ask them to recruit your key personnel,* to be hired on a contract basis for the first six months until you can evaluate their suitability. Employment in Japan is a long-term commitment and your company must be very careful to hire only the best—and most loyal—people. This is more difficult than you may suppose, as many experienced Japanese men are reluctant to work for foreign companies—they know there will not be lifetime security, and afterwards they can't get back into the stratified Japanese business system. Fortunately, younger Japanese men and Japanese women are less fearful and some may see an opportunity with a foreign company as a decided advantage.

Professional personnel specialists can be a great help in your recruiting, but your company must provide specific requirements. Some personnel consultants interview applicants in the applicants' homes. This is not unusual in Japan, where the family is considered very much a part of the "working team." It also gives the personnel consultant a chance to evaluate a prospective employee in his home environment.

All top Japanese companies have the right connections in universities to help them hire the best graduates. This is part of their highly developed information network. Foreign companies, who lack equally sophisticated networks, must work extra hard to compete in finding top-quality personnel. It is never too soon for your Japanese company to start establishing personal contacts at Japanese universities with those professors who train graduates in your company's special field. Your manager should know that a directory of companies' recruiting needs is circulated on most major Japanese college campuses; your company may wish to be included. One of your manager's primary responsibilities, therefore, should be to begin building networks in Japan. Without them, your company cannot succeed.

While your manager is busy building his Japanese networks, your company might consider some *nemawashi* in the United States. Our own pool of Japanese language specialists is frequently overlooked. American universities and language schools can be consulted and you can alert them to your need for Japanese-speaking personnel. Any American company that can send personnel to Japan who already know the language has a tremendous advantage. Americans who can speak Japanese can communicate more effectively with their Japanese staff; they can find housing and settle their families with much less time, effort, and expense than would otherwise be required.

There already exist a number of Japanologists, specialists who have degrees in Japanese history, economics, language, and culture from such major universities as Harvard, Yale, Cornell, Columbia, Stanford, and the University of California. Graduate departments at these and other universities can provide lists of their graduates. Another source of expertise in Japan is the pool of retired Foreign Service officers as well as retired personnel from other international government agencies who have served in Japan. Sad to report, an American executive who attended the University of Tokyo in the 1960s told us that among his friends at *Todai* were a number of Americans studying to be Japanologists with the goal of finding jobs with American industry. But American companies were not interested in Japanologists at the time. Most of his friends were unsuccessful and eventually had to give up and enter the teaching profession.

WHEN THINGS GO WRONG

When things go wrong, as they inevitably will, it is important to be able to recognize the signs and to draw back. Do not try to fix things on the spot. Let the Japanese drive to maintain harmonious relations do its work.

What do we mean by "when things go wrong"? Answer: when people become visibly upset. This can happen at the most unexpected times and under the most surprising circumstances. Once, while we were staying at one of Tokyo's finest hotels, we sent a telex to our office in New Mexico. After some time, it became clear that the telex had not been delivered. In trying to discover what had happened, where the slip-up had occurred, our only point of contact was the hotel telex office. Foreseeing chances for misunderstanding, and mindful of all the foreigners we had seen and heard raising their voices and pounding on desks, we made our approach with caution and trepidation, in a low-key manner, accompanied by a Japanese friend to do the talking. Even so, the clerk thought we were accusing him of error. He became visibly distressed, and nothing we said reassured him. For the moment his mind was closed to our protestations that the fault clearly lay with the New Mexico telex office. What to do? First, even though the New Mexico telex office was the culprit, we apologized. Then, conferring with our Japanese intermediary, we asked if a gift would help. The gift did not have to be expensive, since it was the gesture that was important. The next day a small present, appropriately wrapped, was presented during a quiet time of the morning so there would be no distractions. The man's injured ego was repaired and good relations were reestablished.

Why was all this time and trouble necessary? We weren't at fault. He wasn't at fault. It was simply a misunderstanding. We had done our best to avoid bad feelings. When this sort of incident occurs (and it will if you stay long enough), there are three things to remember: (1) the Japanese transaction rules have been violated (even though inadvertently); (2) the person of superior status is obliged to set things to rights; (3) establishing who is to blame is irrelevant; what is wrong is that someone is upset, and that is what must be corrected.

It is a waste of time to try to fix blame, which Americans almost inevitably do as part of our confrontational, litigious style. What matters in Japan is to repair the damage, to make people feel good again, to establish harmony. Being able to show contrition, to say that one is sorry when the other person is upset, is vital. The telex incident may seem trivial, but to the man behind the desk it was not trivial. Our reason for giving this simple example is that it illustrates many factors present in more complex situations where the stakes are much higher. The best rule to follow is to have a Japanese friend who can intervene, who can provide advice and counsel, and whose networks are sufficiently powerful to be able to help you in a critical situation.

A much more difficult situation is one in which a Japanese crucial to the success of an operation is upset yet doesn't show it. This is a common occurrence. It is essential that Americans learn to read the subtle signs of reluctance or distress or anger and keep up to date through networks on the latest information on people's feelings. Some indications of reluctance or distress are when requests are not acted upon; when the person replies, "I will do my best"; or when he sucks in his breath, looks doubtful, and says "Sah. . . ." Anger is hard to perceive in the Japanese, as they tend to hide it and become more contained than usual and rigid in posture (as if they were holding in their rage). They may drop their voice and speak very softly and slowly or become tight-lipped.

COMMUNICATION AND NEGOTIATION

TIME: FLEXIBILITY AND
SHIFTING SYSTEMS

 Most Americans, as we've seen, are monochronic both in business and at home. Scheduling and agendas are their principal tools for organizing life. In polychronic Japan, the bullet trains run practically on the second, and appointments are kept promptly, but decisions take forever. The key to understanding Japanese time is to know that the Japanese have two modes: a monochronic mode for foreigners and technology and a polychronic mode for virtually everything else.

The Japanese switch from an open system for those in their inner circle to a more closed and tightly scheduled system for outsiders. Therefore, the foreigner's first impression is that everything in Japan is rigidly scheduled. The Japanese have been known to treat a foreign visitor's time as a trunk to be packed, and the tighter the better. They organize his time for him and present him a full schedule upon his arrival.

However, as one comes to know the Japanese and remains in the country longer than a few days, one discovers another aspect of their time system: flexibility. Often, after an ap-

pointment has been arranged, there will be mutual adjustments, postponements, and compromises to fit everyone's
needs.

Another facet of Japanese time is the division into propitious and nonpropitious times. In their correspondence the
Japanese use greetings appropriate for each season of the
year. Just as plants grow and flower, when it comes to decision-making the seasonal clock may be a more appropriate
measuring instrument than the one on the wall or the calen-
dar. No one knows exactly how long a decision will take, and
until everyone has been consulted, agrees, and is behind the
plan, until cooperation is assured up and down the line,
nothing can happen.

The historical past is important to Japanese and they take it
for granted that the visitor will be familiar with the main
points of Japanese history. One hears frequent references to
the Meiji period and to the periods surrounding the Toku-
gawa restoration. These references frequently contain important contexting clues as to how your interlocutor is thinking.

It is advisable not only to know the past but to be well
informed about every aspect of the situation in which you will
be working. When dealing with the Japanese, you must keep
in mind that many important things are frequently left unsaid.
The foreigner in Japan is working in an information-rich environment and must learn to develop readily available means
for tapping the multiple information sources.

When the Japanese are dealing with foreigners they are apt
to seem extremely low-context and to require detailed, technical information, almost as though there were no context at
all, as in programming a computer. This is because they need
to be totally informed, and in a new situation will need to
make their own synthesis of the data. They will also take
everything you say seriously, even jokes. There are times
when this orientation can be time-consuming and vexing,
such as when a rough sketch designed to give the Japanese

client the main drift of an advertising campaign is rejected because it is taken for the finished product.

MEETINGS: GETTING TO KNOW YOU

"To succeed in Japan you must understand the difference between being efficient and being effective."

Management consultant in Tokyo

◄ ◄► ►

In the United States, as we have seen, the function of meetings is to complete the agenda, which is presented in written form at the beginning of the meeting. The agenda is organized in logical sequence, and the chair tries to restrict discussion to items on the agenda and to keep discussions short and to the point. Japanese meetings don't have a fixed agenda. Their purpose is to listen carefully to everyone's input, discuss alternative solutions to each problem presented, and eventually reach a consensus as to priorities. The goal is to encourage the presentation of diverse points of view and at times the discussion can become heated. But everyone works toward adjustments and compromise at every stage. There are no winners or losers. All conflicts must be resolved to everyone's satisfaction to insure harmonious group interaction, and the Japanese spend whatever time is necessary to achieve this.

When the Japanese meet with foreigners, the most important thing on their agenda is to get to know them. They are quite expert at determining what tactics are effective with foreigners and will try various strategies to see what works. They also ask many probing questions, testing your knowledge of your facts and your sincerity and conviction. Japanese admire people who are serious about their work, well informed, sincere, and honest. Long before there can be any discussion of substantive issues, the Japanese want to have some understanding of and feeling for the *people* involved. It is very important not to be impatient during this phase. If you deny the Japanese this opportunity to become acquainted, you will not succeed in substantive matters.

NEGOTIATIONS: EVERYBODY WINS SOMETHING

Most American companies send people to negotiate who are woefully unprepared. They know little about Japan and even less about the art of Japanese negotiations. Americans tend to approach negotiations as a game which they are determined to win. In Japan everybody must win.

For concrete examples of the enormous cost to American business of sending people to Japan who are unprepared, spend a week having breakfast in the coffee shop at any of the major hotels in Tokyo. You will see and hear several groups of American businessmen who arrive on Monday and expect to "have it wrapped up by Friday." It's like attending a play which repeats the first act over and over. You soon know the script and you can predict the results. By Wednesday the Americans are angry and by Friday they are both furious and anxious about how they will explain their failure to the home office. These fruitless meetings and negotiations cost American companies thousands of dollars for each person they send to Japan. We observed many groups of Americans having such discussions during one recent five-week visit. It was very discouraging.

When you are choosing a Japanese partner and are about to enter into negotiations, you will need at least two key people to assist you. Here are a few general suggestions for selecting them, based on our own experience and that of the people we interviewed.

First, you will need an experienced go-between, someone of suitable status and reputation. To find him you will need the assistance of your bankers and your other connections in Japan. You will also need a highly trained, skilled Japanese interpreter, someone with an excellent education and high intelligence, who is able to use the Japanese language with exactly the right degree of politeness to put other Japanese at ease. Take ample time (a minimum of two hours, and all day or longer if need be) to brief your interpreter thoroughly about your business. Be sure to inform the interpreter about the key points you expect to discuss. We cannot overemphasize the critical role of these two figures, the go-between and the interpreter; the success of your negotiations may well depend on how effectively they represent you.

The art of negotiation involves two key Japanese concepts: *tatemae* and *honne*. *Tatemae* means "front face," what is presented. It involves form—the formal principles of polite behavior accepted by all Japanese to insure harmony and good feelings. *Honne* means substance, your real intent, and your personal feelings, which are rarely divulged. All discussion of *honne* involves *tatemae*. Directly related is "saving face."

Courtesy calls between the president, or another official from your company, and his exact counterpart in the hierarchy of the Japanese firm are very important, rather like a state visit. Even if other executives in your organization will be charged with the actual negotiations, the top officials of both companies should meet. This formal greeting ceremony is termed *aisatsu,* a ritual that precedes negotiations.

> "If the Japanese don't feel right about you, they will not do business with you."
>
> Japanese company president

◄ ◄ ► ►

CASE HISTORY: One of Tokyo's leading management consultants, an American whom we will call Smith, received a call from a Japanese client who had been approached by an American company wanting to purchase his business. The Japanese, Mori, wanted Smith to accompany him to the meetings with the Americans. At the beginning of the first meeting, after introductions had been made, Mori stood and gave a formal speech of welcome to the Americans—the CEO of the American company, two other officers, and their attorney. Mori invited all of them to a luncheon and also to a dinner that evening. He closed by expressing his best wishes for a pleasant visit in Japan. Smith then translated Mori's speech for the Americans, who had not brought an interpreter to the meeting.

The American reply was given by the CEO: "We are here to negotiate. We're leaving Friday on Pan Am and here's the game plan. We will discuss specifics, our attorney is with us and the sooner we get down to business the better."

Smith, who was playing a double role as translator and go-between, was distressed. He could not translate the American's remarks literally without insulting Mori. However, Smith did manage to convey the desire of the Americans for an immediate discussion of substantive issues. Mori sucked in his breath and then he stood up again and gave the exact same speech of welcome he had given earlier, reiterating his invitations for luncheon and dinner. When this was translated the Americans refused both invitations and said they would return after lunch.

Two days of fruitless discussions followed with no sign of agreement or rapprochement. Each day the Americans declined Mori's invitations to dinner saying they had to telephone New York during the evening. Whenever discussion centered on specifics, the American attorney would take notes frantically and then leave the meeting to telex the company. Whenever discussion veered he tapped his pen on the table, muttering, "Time is money." By the end of the third day, both sides were discouraged and the Americans were enraged at the lack of progress. Finally, the Americans broke off the negotiations and left to go home.

◄ ◄► ►

The irony in all this was that Mori really wanted to sell his business, but first he had to know something about the prospective buyers as human beings. He wanted some feeling for what kind of people they were. Failing to understand this need, the Americans resisted every attempt to get together informally with the Japanese, to relax after work and have a good time over dinner and an evening on the town. This would have provided an opportunity to begin building a relationship, but the Americans considered such socializing a waste of time.

PRESENTATIONS:
LOGIC VS. INDIRECTION

Americans try to be orderly in outlining their facts and in summarizing their main points. For Japanese, the end of a communication is not as important as a propitious beginning. Most important, they consider the practice of ordering facts for others comparable to tying a child's shoelaces for him after the child has already learned the skill. In general, high-context people in their own environment don't like to be told how to do things, including how to order their facts. European logic is perceived as intrusive by Japanese, as an attempt to get inside other people's heads and do their thinking for them. The Japanese would no more do that than they would rearrange the furniture in someone else's house or office. Surprisingly enough, when the Japanese do ask for information, it will probably be for information that is more detailed and diverse than Americans are used to providing, because the Japanese want *all* the facts, not just a special selection. While the Japanese dig deeply into information, they prefer to order the data themselves in a manner different from the American way of thinking.

This difference relates to logic. Logic is a mode of thinking invented by the early Greeks that is integral to the Europeans and Americans, but is anathema to the Japanese. They feel that "logical," linear, one-step-at-a-time arguments denote immaturity. The Japanese have their own very powerful modes of thought, their own systems of logic. A professor at the University of Kyoto explained the difference to us. He started by saying that there are at least two forms of logic in the world: linear logic and that which goes by the Japanese name of *okeya ronri*. *Okeya ronri* is illustrated by the saying, "When the wind blows it is good for the makers of wooden tubs." The logic in this very high-context metaphor goes something like this: The wind kicks up dust and sand and makes people uncomfortable and depressed. To overcome their depression, they play a stringed instrument called the *shamisen*, much used in early times. The strings of the *shamisen* are made of catgut. Therefore, people kill cats in order to string their *shamisens*, and the resulting reduction in the number of cats leads to a proliferation of mice. The mice gnaw at the tubs in which grain is stored, which in turn increases the demand for wooden grain-storage tubs. Hence, "When the wind blows it is good for the makers of wooden tubs." The story may seem farfetched to Americans, but it expresses quite accurately the Japanese preoccupation with being able to see the long-term implications of actions as well as the relationships between apparently unrelated systems.

"Many messages are not only minimal but actually obscure as well so that the success of communication depends as much on the sensitivity of its recipient as on the quality of the message sent. . . . All members of a group expect their unstated feelings to be understood and their unarticulated desires to be anticipated."

Robert J. Smith, *Japanese Society*

"The more important the matter being discussed, the more indirect the Japanese manner of communication will be."

Mark Zimmerman, *How to Do Business with the Japanese*

◄◄►►

The typical American manner of presentation can be a problem. Americans communicate directly and look at the other person when they speak. They come right to the point and ask direct questions. These highly valued communication styles are unnerving to the Japanese, whose whole manner is marked by indirection. They are made uncomfortable by Americans who look at them directly; they choose to look down or at the corner of the room. Japanese try to gather information without asking direct questions, and they talk around a subject. For Japanese, frankness and bluntness are taboo; even exactness is to be avoided because it is considered arrogant and impertinent. This manner creates difficulties for the more impatient Americans, as it takes time to discover things simply by watching and listening. The American in Japan is likely to ask himself, "Why beat around the bush? Why not come straight out and say what's on your mind? They are going to find out anyway, so why waste time?" The point is, by saving time in the short term, less information is shared, the relationship suffers, and long-term goals are threatened.

It is interesting and somewhat paradoxical that the American communication style is direct and to the point, yet we were told repeatedly that Americans talk too much and do not know how to listen. Americans must learn to pay close attention to the Japanese and pick up the subtle, nonverbal cues in conversation, such as a slight tilt of the head when there is a negative reaction.

An important point that must be stressed has to do with what sociologist Erving Goffman calls "the presentation of self." The presentation of self in the two countries starts from radically different points of view. The American is concerned with himself and with his performance; he wants to "make things happen." The Japanese is concerned about himself primarily in his relationship to his group; above all, he wants to maintain harmony.

The American tries to project a facade of confidence. Over the centuries, the Japanese have developed X-ray vision for seeing behind this facade; in fact, they are quite adept at detecting even minute differences between the facade an individual projects to the outside world and what he is really thinking or feeling. While it is true that Japanese are apt to misread messages in cross-cultural situations, in the long run it is impossible to fool them. Don't even try. As one industrialist observed, "There are times when you must *feel* tough, because if they sense underlying weakness, you are lost."

The Japanese are well aware of the fact that the face they display to the world at large may be quite different from what they are feeling inside or from the face they display at home. For the Japanese, their facade is defined situationally and follows the dictates of custom for various relationships.

It is absolutely essential to learn to read the meaning of specific actions in any foreign country. The most natural mistake a foreigner makes is to read into a strange culture meanings from his own, an action that can lead to serious miscueing and misunderstandings. For example, when the Japanese say yes, they may not mean yes. To the Japanese, "Yes" simply means "I hear you." Never assume that they agree, especially in business discussions. Also, do not assume that a smile means the Japanese are pleased or are agreeing with you, since they often smile or laugh when embarrassed.

SAVING FACE: THE KEY TO SUCCESSFUL INTERACTIONS

Saving face is very important to the Japanese. It is the key to preserving harmony, not only in business relations but in personal relations as well.

In negotiations, saving face is of paramount importance. You must:

1. *Listen, listen, listen* and then listen some more.
2. *Present a total picture* of your objectives in which everything is interrelated. The Japanese don't like bits and pieces.
3. *Stress areas of agreement* whenever possible and build on them.
4. *Never ask questions unless you are sure they can be answered.* Instead, give the Japanese your questions ahead of time so they can prepare their answers and thereby not lose face.
5. *Never reject or refuse a proposal outright.* Say you will consider it. Later, if you decide to refuse, do it very politely, make apologies, and give all your reasons.

Negotiations with foreigners are serious business for the Japanese. Their strong drive for consensus within their own society and their own company does not necessarily extend to negotiations with outsiders. Be prepared to play "hardball," but do it with politeness and style. When the Japanese yield on a point, large or small, they will present it as a magnanimous gesture on their part. Let them say so, and show your appreciation. They will expect you to make a concession, too. It's part of their philosophy of give-and-take.

6. *Insist on discussing long-term generalized goals first.* Only after these have been agreed on can you begin discussion of specifics (cost, price, etc.). It is helpful to distribute ahead of time a memo of items to be discussed so the Japanese can prepare themselves. This is not an agenda; the meeting will not proceed like an American meeting.

7. *Be patient.* Impatience is perceived by the Japanese as weakness. Therefore, you must never act impatient. Try not to fidget, jiggle your feet, play with your pen, tap your pencil, cross and uncross your legs, sigh, or exhibit other signs of impatience. These actions will be interpreted by the Japanese as a sign of bad manners or a lack of sincere interest on your part.

8. *Avoid commitments to deadlines or dates of departure.* Otherwise, you will simply throw away your advantage, because the Japanese will use this deadline as a lever. It's a good idea to announce at the beginning that you are prepared to stay until you reach a successful conclusion.

9. *Be receptive to invitations* to dine, play golf, or visit places of historic interest.

10. *Be polite.* Attention to etiquette is very important. Learn to disagree without being disagreeable. Never confront; don't shout, don't pound the table, and don't shake your finger at anyone; the Japanese will lose respect for you. Remind yourself that uncontrolled emotion is considered a sign of weakness and poor taste.

11. *Avoid rigid adherence to logic.* We realize this is very

difficult for Americans, but formal Western logic does not move the Japanese.

12. *Be aware of feelings and emotions* and base your approach on them, because the Japanese are sensitive and will respond to this. Japanese depend heavily on nonverbal communication and are very sensitive to it. As one executive said, "Sometimes I think they can read my mind."

13. *Don't complain.* The Japanese consider this whining.

14. *Don't try to bargain.* This makes the Japanese uncomfortable and insecure. They like persuasion, not pressure.

15. *Be prepared for silence.* The Japanese like to sit back and reflect. They don't feel people have to talk all the time. It doesn't mean they are giving you "the silent treatment" or getting upset or angry; it's simply part of their language of interaction. Periods of silence are very important and should not be broken. Use the time to reflect and enjoy the pauses. The Japanese say, "Eloquence is silver. Silence is gold."

CASE HISTORY: In the midst of negotiations with an American company, the Japanese in charge of negotiations for his company listened intently to the American presentation and the translation that followed. Then, the Japanese leaned back to think about the proposal, rocked back and forth very slowly for a moment and finally reached into his pocket for a cigarette, which he tapped on the table. The Americans became uncomfortable at the long silence, and one of them began speaking. This occurred several times during their meeting and the result was that, each time the Japanese was ready to respond, the Americans interrupted him, breaking his action chain, because they didn't recognize signs of impending response.

16. *Pay close attention to what the Japanese are doing in negotiations.* Give them lots of time. There will be many pauses in the meetings. Some Japanese require a long time to get "wound up" before they talk; they like to warm up first. If they don't have a chance to participate at their own pace, they cannot establish a relationship.

17. *Remember that inscrutability is not deception.* If you cannot understand their reactions or feelings, do not be misled and attribute this to their being deceptive.

18. *Be thoroughly prepared* with hard data, facts, and figures about everything the Japanese will need to know. In other words, "Don't wing it." The Japanese need for information often goes far beyond what most Americans expect.

CASE HISTORY: After nearly four weeks of negotiation one American CEO, who had been doing business in Japan for thirty years with great success, finally decided to break off negotiations for a new venture.

At the next meeting he thanked the Japanese profusely for their patience and goodwill and told them how much he had enjoyed getting to know them and how much he had wanted to do business with them. He added he had decided very reluctantly that the two sides just could not reach agreement. He invited them to reconsider his last proposal and to meet with him one more time, the following evening at his hotel.

When the Japanese arrived, he offered them refreshments and they sat around talking informally. Then he asked them if they had anything further to say after reviewing his last proposal. When they said no, he got up, went around to each Japanese, shook hands and thanked him for his efforts, and said goodbye. He then opened the closet door, picked up his bags, and left to get the limousine to the airport. The Japanese were not expecting this.

Upon his arrival in Los Angeles, he was greeted by three top staff of the Japanese company, who asked him to return to Japan immediately for further talks. He did so, and the negotiations were successfully completed.

◄ ◄► ►

This happy ending may not always occur, but there is definitely a point when negotiations are no longer productive and it is best to end them gracefully. Just don't give up too soon and don't be impolite. In this case the American CEO knew many of the Japanese and had worked with them for years. He was sufficiently contexted to know when to leave.

Finally, bear in mind that in negotiations matters of major substance may be referred back to Japanese company headquarters for decision. As you'll remember from our discussion of the *ringi*, major decisions take a very long time in Japan.

CONTRACTS AND ATTORNEYS

". . . you can indeed have understanding without agreement, but you can never, ever, have any agreement without understanding."

Don Maloney, "East Is East—Or Is It?"

◄ ◄► ►

Americans, oriented to the printed word, prefer written agreements. They think contracts are final and legally binding. This is not the case in Japan. Quite often, after a contract has been signed, the Japanese will request a meeting at which they ask for changes, which usually means the American company representative in Japan must contact U.S. headquarters for approval. The American reaction is one of indignation or distress because Americans regard a contract as binding, a stable element in a changing and uncertain world. Many Japanese contracts have a clause that says if the situation changes the contract will be renegotiated. Even if the clause is not there, they will expect to renegotiate if the situation changes. For the Japanese, if conditions change, everything changes. This is particularly true if there is a change in the exchange rate or a rise in the price of oil.

For the Japanese a verbal agreement is just as binding as a written agreement. Be warned, and *never* commit yourself to saying something you don't mean. Apart from your need to consult attorneys about patents and trademarks, however, you will not need the services of an attorney in Japan nearly as often as you would in Europe or the United States. Japan is not a litigious society and prefers to work things out harmoniously through negotiation.

There are many restrictions imposed on foreign attorneys who wish to practice in Japan. First, there are long delays in obtaining a visa. Then, there is the requirement that the foreign attorney must pass the bar exam and also pass a language competency test. This helps explain why in 1984 there were only approximately twenty foreign attorneys licensed to practice in Japan.

Due to a shortage of judges, Japanese court dockets are very crowded, and it takes years for cases to be settled. In a legal action, if the wrongdoer accepts the blame and makes a public apology, the case is often dropped before it comes to trial. Our interpretation of litigation in Japan, when it occurs, is that, like war, courts are a last resort when all else fails.

MANAGING IN JAPAN

RELATING TO YOUR JAPANESE STAFF

"Keep a light hand on the reins and encourage input and teamwork."

American CEO, Tokyo

友 Shinsaku Sogo, Executive Director of JETRO, writes in his excellent article, "Gaining Respect: The ABCs of How to Get Along With Your Japanese Staff": "Your Japanese staff is not working for you, but for the company." He continues: "In Japan, a company is not merely a functional organization. It is also a cooperative unit." A good manager can enhance this cooperation.

A good Japanese manager is an invaluable asset, so take the time to find one and then listen to him. Keep in mind how important it is to the Japanese to go through channels and to observe the critical chain of command. Rank and status are important and you will lose face if you violate the rules. Your Japanese manager can also assist you in all matters involving customs and Japanese-style communication, thus helping to maintain the constant flow of information on which your organization will depend.

One of the things American management in Japan can do to improve relations with a Japanese staff is to promote company loyalty. The American manager can strengthen feelings of loyalty by observing Japanese customs, such as inducting new employees in a formal ceremony each spring. This induction ceremony promotes solidarity by creating an opportunity for a small celebration, sometimes with music and entertainment. The American manager can use the occasion to ask for the active support of the new employees before beginning their indoctrination into the company. Awards to groups for outstanding performance (for instance, as a QCC) are also helpful.

Company tours also build morale. As mentioned earlier, one highly successful European company arranges annual tours to Germany and France with visits to the company facilities as well as sightseeing and entertainment. Other foreign companies offer children of Japanese employees an opportunity to go to their country and study in their schools. This builds bridges with the Japanese families, and it encourages Japanese children to develop their language skills.

Learning to communicate effectively with Japanese staff is very important. One great difference between American and Japanese business is in how office communications are handled. Americans use written communications, procedures, and memos which are circulated within the office. The Japanese are not accustomed to this. They communicate verbally. Remember they are tied to information networks based on close personal relationships and constantly keep each other informed. Ask your Japanese advisor how best to communicate with the Japanese in your office.

If a difficult personnel problem arises, it is important to find a solution before the problem becomes public. For example, if an employee has failed to do his job or if he has been dishonest, this must be dealt with promptly and quietly, in private. You must have advice from top Japanese staff on this. It is very difficult to fire an employee. However, for serious infractions it can be done.

For less serious offenses, never reprimand or make accusations in public. It will embarrass the person and it will ruin your relationship. If you have a grievance, discuss it in private with great tact. Always begin by stressing the positive. When you broach the deficiency in his work, make one or two diplomatic and vague suggestions. Ask him to think about the matter and discuss it with you later. Even better, *find a go-between to speak to the employee.*

THE IMPORTANCE OF
AFTER-HOURS SOCIALIZING

As noted, one of the most important parts of doing business in Japan is after-hours socializing. For your staff this kind of socializing is one of the major channels of communication. This is when you find out what is really going on, when the barriers come down, when you can say things without offense. Bear in mind that during the day office etiquette prevents any exchanges that might be considered improper or offensive. The pressure to keep a tight rein on emotions is very great. In the words of one American advertising executive, "The Japanese don't trust anyone who doesn't go out and drink with them."

PROBLEMS WITH THE HOME OFFICE

Most American executives we interviewed in Japan said one of their biggest problems was with their home office. It was often the first thing they mentioned. Because American business is conducted so differently from Japanese business it is very difficult to convey to the home office the reality of doing business in Japan. Most U.S. headquarters don't understand and often refuse to accept the advice and recommen-

dations of their top managers in Japan when this advice jus
doesn't make sense to them. Often they insist that specific
company policies and procedures be applied worldwide. We
were often told: "You cannot tell headquarters anything.
They refuse to listen and it has cost this company hundreds of
thousands of dollars!" (Some executives said "millions of
dollars.")

Our experience has been that problems between the home
office and the overseas operation are not restricted to American business. We heard the same complaints from French and
German business executives abroad. It is also true for American government agencies. Many Foreign Service officers reported that the FSO abroad is always thinking about "the
department"—the desk officer at State—who reads his reports and decides whether or not to act on them.

Visits by company brass sometimes pose dilemmas for the
American executive in Japan. In the words of one American
banker:

> "The problem is, the wrong people come. If the
> right people do come they don't stay long enough
> to learn anything. All too often it's a junket and
> they bring their wives along. This means we cannot
> have important after-hours meetings with our Japa-
> nese clients. My advice is to send top people who
> are really interested in Japan and give them at least
> a week and preferably two."

When wives accompany their husbands on these visits, our
suggestion is that their visit be scheduled separately and they
be offered an orientation course on Japan and tours to such
places as Kyoto, Nara, or Nikko. Many organizations offer
such orientation; one that specializes in arrangements for
business wives is Oak Associates in Tokyo. Many wives are
interested in learning about Japan, and sometimes educating
wives is a very good way to reach husbands, especially when

their husbands feel they don't have time to absorb the culture.

Another problem with the home office, often mentioned in our interviews, is that of telexes from the home office. In the words of one frustrated American CEO:

> "Americans send terrible telexes. They can't write clearly—they use jargon and slang which baffles the Japanese. They are sometimes tactless and don't think how something will sound. They think a telex is like a cable and the more you leave out the better. Take this example: 'Here's new data sheet. Please throw away.' What they meant, of course, was 'Please throw away the old one.'"

MARKETING, SELLING, AND DISTRIBUTING

MARKETING: LEARNING FROM THE MASTERS

"What sells in the United States does not necessarily sell in Japan. But the concept can be transferred with intelligent interpretation and translation."

Kenichi Ohmae, *Triad Power*

 The Japanese are the world's most sophisticated marketers. To succeed in Japan a product must be unique, of very high quality, and adapted to the needs and preferences of the Japanese. Most important, deliveries must be prompt, in accordance with the tight scheduling of the Japanese. The Japanese market is the second largest in the world and is fiercely competitive. Only high-quality products that are competitive in price have a chance. America's biggest single problem in the Japanese marketplace is the uneven quality of American products.

In order to be able to turn out quality products at affordable prices, many Japanese producers have invested heavily in automated plants. Several years ago a major American company developed a high-quality robot. The manager, an American, presented it at a trade show in Tokyo and, in his words, "The Japanese were climbing over the ropes to get at it and attendance skyrocketed." The company decided to market the robot in the United States after trying it out on an assembly line in an American plant. The U.S. workers, fearful for their jobs, sabotaged the robot. The American manufacturer then withdrew it from the market and refused to move the robot manufacturing operation to Japan, despite the urging of the manager in Japan. The company then sold the patent because "it had no future." The Japanese buyer, believing otherwise, continued to develop the robot, adding several sophisticated features with great success.

Mariko Fujiwara has written an excellent book on consumer preferences in Japan, *Hitonami: Keeping Up with the Satos*. It is must reading for companies producing consumer goods. JETRO and the American Chamber of Commerce in Japan can provide basic market information. If your company requires more detailed information, your bankers and your Japanese associates can arrange for the proper introductions to reliable market research companies. Top-level contacts are needed for these introductions. If your company is not affiliated with a Japanese company, it is particularly important to rely on a professional market research firm. Conducting market research in Japan is very difficult for foreigners and is a highly specialized field.

Because the Japanese market is highly volatile and subject to great swings, companies must stay abreast of changes in their industry's marketplace. In 1986 the market for imported cars was quite strong. The newly affluent middle-class Japanese wanted high-status fashionable cars that met their need for individuality. Some foreign car companies, such as BMW, reduced their prices and lowered interest rates to take advantage of this trend in the market.

Proper placement is an important factor and can become

part of the sales promotion. The fact that an item such as cosmetics is in a first-class department store is very important for status. If one important store carries a product, others will follow.

Many Japanese have a special feeling of attachment to their appliances. Marketing expert George Field thinks this is related to the physical space the appliances occupy in Japanese homes. Japanese homes and apartments are very small and the television and the washing machine become a part of the home environment. Often both are found in the living room with the family.

Service for appliances is important. Japanese expect to find skilled repair shops in their neighborhood able to fix anything they buy. Incidentally, we were told one of the best ways to become an accepted member of your neighborhood is to get to know the local repair people and their shops.

Packaging must be beautiful and of high quality. The Japanese avoid any product that is presented in "economy packaging." They also dislike certain colors for certain products: they abhor yellow for cosmetics or toilet articles because they associate yellow with laundry or cleaning products. This is just one example of why you need the input of local advertising specialists.

The Japanese housewife makes most of the major purchases for the family and buys the family's food, household supplies, and clothing. Usually, she receives her husband's paycheck, manages the household budget, and allocates funds for different categories of expenses, including savings for children's education, vacations, leisure activities, and retirement. She is the person advertisers try to reach. She budgets carefully and is an informed and astute shopper, often keeping daily records of her purchases.

The Japanese themselves are careful to design their products around people's needs. One of the great challenges for foreign companies is adapting foreign products to Japanese eeds. Braun, for example, had to redesign its electric shaver to fit the smaller hands of Japanese customers. Other companies, such as Sears, reduced the size of their home appliances to fit the needs of Japanese consumers, who live in small spaces. These simple adaptations can spell the difference between success and failure.

Consider Japanese needs in automobiles, for example. The Japanese need a car with right-hand drive because they drive on the left side of the road. This sounds obvious, yet many American and European car manufacturers have refused to make this adaptation, which has cost them thousands of sales. The Japanese also need air conditioning for driving in cities such as Tokyo, where the climate is hot in summer and traffic is jammed. Because they do not have superhighways and their streets and roads are very congested, Japanese like small, highly responsive cars with power steering for parking in tight spaces.

> "At some point American business and government leaders will face the fact that we are losing the trade war with Japan (and other Asian nations) because we don't know how to sell to them, because our army of marketers are undertrained and unsupported by their companies."
>
> —John L. Graham, "Today the Summit—Tomorrow, Business"

ADVERTISING: RELEASING
THE RIGHT RESPONSE

Each nation and each culture has its own way of describing its products and the company behind the products. These stylistic variations evolved through a natural process of interaction between advertisers, media, and the marketplace. The function of all advertising is to *release a desired response.*

Japanese advertising evokes a mood and is designed to appeal to emotions, produce good feelings, and create a happy atmosphere. The approach is a "soft sell." Japanese ads are visually attractive and eye-catching, featuring bright colors. This fits the Japanese visual orientation to life and reflects their sensitivity to aesthetics, color, and design. They often use symbols and strong gestures in their TV commercials. Japanese ads may be humorous or witty, and they appeal to the reader's intelligence; however, they do not convey much product information. The Japanese culture is so high-context that the ads need not be filled with information. Japanese ads seem to violate all the American rules for good advertising; in fact, sometimes it's hard to discern what the product is from viewing a Japanese ad.

The Japanese consumer is very aware of trends and wants the latest fashions in consumer products. Well-known personalities are "opinion leaders" in Japan. The Japanese tend to imitate famous people and buy the products that they endorse. Celebrities, such as film stars and famous athletes, are often shown promoting products in both TV and print ads.

For consumer products, in the words of one advertising specialist:

> "I tell my clients, if you want to do something—do it big! Lots of ads and the best possible placement in leading department stores. You want to project an image of quality and prestige."

Data sheets are very important because the Japanese expect information in great detail about the products they buy. Simply translating American product information will not suffice because Japanese organize information very differently. Hire well-educated, experienced Japanese to write data sheets; they are too important to be assigned to amateurs.

Some advertising agencies create product-information literature as part of their service to clients.

The Japanese family averages five hours a day watching TV. Television advertising is therefore important and very expensive. There are five commercial channels in Tokyo that broadcast all day, from early morning until late at night. Early morning hours are most important for advertisers.

In 1983 the percentages of total advertising expenditure were as follows: TV, 34.6 percent; newspapers, 30.1 percent; magazines, 6.2 percent; radio, 5.1 percent; and outdoor, direct mail, and others, 24.0 percent. Since so many Japanese take mass transit to work, ads on trains and subways are very popular.

The Japanese magazine market is highly segmented. There are more than 2,740 different *categories* of highly specialized magazines. For example, in the area of girls' magazines there are those for virtually every age: young girls 10–12, girls 12–14, 14–16, etc. The fine distinctions in readership segmentation exceed anything we have encountered in other countries.

CASE HISTORY: After forty years of publishing a Japanese edition, an American magazine decided to close its Japanese subsidiary. Six years of losses preceded this decision. Once a very popular magazine in Japan, its circulation had dropped while production costs rose. According to Susan Chira in the New York *Times*, the head of the company union stated in an interview that the company "brought on its own trouble by failing to adapt its product to changing Japanese tastes and by using direct-mail marketing tactics that did not appeal to the Japanese, such as the sweepstakes approach."

◄ ◄›►

American companies will need input from Japanese experts on where to place ads to target consumers accurately.

CASE HISTORY: An American company's headquarters, disregarding the advice of its Tokyo manager, decided to advertise its product in English in six publications in Southeast Asia. The ads were designed to reach Japanese business and there was a coupon attached. The company received not one reply. American headquarters couldn't understand this. Yet any knowledgeable advertising agency could have told them that none of these six magazines is read by the Japanese, and this information could have saved the company thousands of dollars.

◄ ◄›►

Some of the best advertising agencies in the world are in Tokyo. Two of the largest Japanese agencies are well known: Dentsu and Hakuhodo. There are also many smaller Japanese agencies and American agencies, some of which are joint ventures with the Japanese. It is not difficult to find a good agency, and it will be time well spent to investigate several of them.

The advertising business in Japan is totally different from that in the United States. Japanese ad agencies specialize in a particular medium. They also handle competing clients.

PUBLIC RELATIONS

Japanese have little concept of public relations in the American sense; they find American public relations incomnensible. Since they are very modest and self-effacing, ey cannot understand self-promotion. They also have little need for corporate public relations. There is an old saying in Japan: "The peach tree and the plum tree say nothing, but when the fruit is ripe everybody comes."

SALES: TIME WELL SPENT

The Japanese salesman serves as a public relations representative for his company. As you may imagine, he spends many hours with his good customers. He does not wait for customers to call him or come into his store or office. He makes frequent calls in person, and he may not even mention his products or attempt a sale. Instead, he will visit with his customer, dine with him, go to *sake* bars, play golf or tennis, and get to know him. He serves his customer in any way he can and builds a long-term relationship which may well last a lifetime.

When he does make a sales call on a customer he never gets right to the point. First, he visits and spends a long time in pleasant conversation. Eventually, he gets down to business. For some Americans this may seem a waste of time, but in Japan it is not. This sales technique is just one example of the cultural difference between being efficient (saving time) and being effective (making a sale).

The responsibility of the company does not end at the point of sale. Free service is expected on products. For example, in orders for heavy machinery, the supplier is responsible for installation, training the operators, maintenance, and service long after the warranty expires. Indeed, many suppliers have automatic check-up inspections for their machinery. This may continue for up to twenty years after purchase. This ongoing inspection serves to cement the relationship as well as to insure proper performance.

American cars have not sold well in Japan. In 1982 only 3,562 U.S.-made cars were sold, and in 1985 only about 9,000. Rosalie Tung attributes this to the fact that American cars are not of high quality and their style and build are not suited to Japanese needs and tastes. Also, we heard many complaints about inadequate service and nonavailability of parts, probably the two most crucial considerations to the Japanese buyer. Most successful foreign automobile companies have encouraged and relied on input from their distributors and salesmen, who talk to customers and know what customers want.

DISTRIBUTION: CRUCIAL NETWORKS

Distribution is handled through a network of independently owned manufacturers' representatives, and products pass through many hands before they are sold. It is very hard for a newcomer to break into the distribution system because of existing franchises which date back many years. This system is often criticized for being both complicated and inefficient. Indeed, some say it is impossible for foreign business to master. At the very least, it is one of the greatest obstacles foreign business confronts. But, as many Japanese point out, it is also very difficult for new Japanese companies, two thirds of which fail.

As you might expect in a high-context culture, the Japanese distribution system is based on a network of personal relationships that may span as many as three generations. These relationships involve years of trust, understanding, and mutual obligation. Not only is the system difficult to understand and break into; it is virtually impossible to explain to the American home office.

The Japanese distribution system is based on reciprocity. It spans many years of working together on the part of buyer and seller. Japanese companies buy from certain suppliers. These, in turn, send the company business or repay the company over the years in some other way. Perhaps, during periods of shortage, they give their clients top priority. This is not considered immoral or illegal; it is simply "helping each other."

Distribution involves both wholesalers and retailers, which are often very small organizations with limited capital and staff. Most small retail stores cannot keep an inventory, and therefore the wholesaler must have supplies that can be delivered on short notice, daily if necessary. The ubiquitous, tiny, family-owned stores are concentrated near commuting stops and along the bus and railroad routes to encourage walk-in customers. These very small stores cannot afford space for large inventories. Similarly, their competitors, the large retail stores that pay high rents, do not want to tie up their capital with large inventories. According to Rosalie Tung, there are 1.5 million retailers in Japan. Seventy-seven percent of total retail sales are in neighborhood stores, not in large department stores. JETRO reports there is one retail store for every seventy-eight people in Japan. This is twice as many per capita as in the United States or France. Only one percent of Japanese retailers employ more than thirty people, and 85 percent have fewer than four employees.

Recently, several very large retail outlets have been started by companies such as Daiei, Nichii, Seiyu, and Ito-Yokado. It is possible for foreign companies to use these retail giants to distribute their products.

Wholesalers are also small and numerous, one for every 468 people. Seventy percent of the wholesalers have fewer than ten employees, and the ratio of wholesalers to retailers is one to five.

On the plus side, the distribution system offers many options and is responsive to changing conditions, an important factor for the Japanese. It requires constant communication and contact between manufacturer, distributor, wholesa... and retailer, and it also requires years of *nemawashi*. Som... times an American company wants to change its distributo... because it isn't satisfied with his performance. This poses problems, because another distributor may not wish to be the "second choice," especially if the company has had problems with its first distributor.

American companies can choose among several distribution options: use a trading company or a Japanese firm to distribute products, at least in the initial stages of your Japanese operation; bypass the distributors and wholesalers and make direct sales to retailers; or sell through wholesalers.

ADVICE FOR AMERICANS

A DISTILLATION OF ADVICE
FROM 50 EXECUTIVES IN JAPAN

"Many American companies are very successful in Japan. It takes a long-term commitment, a lot of money, and good people who are willing to work hard and do it right."

Senior vice-president, American bank in Tokyo

 We were fortunate to have interviewed a number of successful American executives in Japan who were experienced, talented, knowledgeable, and optimistic. The following advice for Americans working in an was given us by these executives, who have learned e hard way how difficult it is to accept the reality of another culture.

FOR INDIVIDUALS

1. *Be patient—very, very patient.* Everything takes much longer in Japan. Major decisions require nine to twelve months. If you are new to your job in Japan, take no major action for eighteen months to two years. It takes five years to begin to understand what is happening. Don't push; consensus takes time. Allow plenty of time for *nemawashi.* Be prepared for many meetings, dinners, evenings out, and weekends with your Japanese associates.

   One executive who started his own business and has been very successful had this to say:

   > "The Japanese like to test your sincerity. I call it the 'jump-through-the-hoop syndrome.' After you've demonstrated repeatedly that you are willing to meet their demands, they continue to ask for more. This is their way of testing you to see if you are sincere and really interested in doing business. This is how you build reputation, by 'jumping through the hoop.' Once the Japanese are satisfied, they will accept you."

2. *Take the long-term view.* The Japanese are not interested in short-term relationships. You must begin by making a long-term plan for your Japanese operation and allow five years just to complete the groundwork.

3. *"Don't come to teach, come to learn."* This was the advice of a long-term resident of Tokyo who is the head of a large trading company.

4. *Learn the language.* Not just our recommendation but that of *everyone* we interviewed.

5. *Learn new ways to communicate.* First, listen carefully and watch for subtle signs of nonverbal communication between Japanese. They do not communicate directly. You can become aware of their feelings by using your own intuition and empathy. This takes practice and coaching. Remember, Western logic is anathema to Japanese. In your communications be *accurate, honest,* and *consistent.* Say only what you mean and be prepared to stand behind what you say.

6. *Respect consensus and compromise.* These are the bases of relationships in Japan. The Japanese achieve harmony by seeking consensus at every level. They compromise when there are differences, and they expect give-and-take and flexibility even from foreigners. If they make a concession, their foreign partner is expected to make one in return.

7. *Accept personal responsibility for your job.* The Japanese expect each member of a firm to be personally responsible for whatever he agrees to do. They are not interested in excuses. In their eyes, you will be held responsible for any commitment.

8. *Be thoroughly prepared.* When you present a proposal the Japanese may not say anything at first. They like time to reflect. But don't think they are not giving your proposal serious consideration. Later, they may come back with questions, questions, and more questions, and requests for additional data. Be prepared and very patient. Japanese will test you over and over again on your facts and figures, and they will probe to see if you are really sincere and honest.

9. *Learn to depend on your Japanese advisors.* You will need coaching and advice every step of the way in Japan, and you must develop a reliable Japanese staff who can advise you. They can give you the best advice in the world, but it won't do any good if you don't

listen and accept that advice. It's a little like the situation you will find yourself in when you try to tell your home office about the Japanese.

10. *Pay great attention to detail.* Most Japanese try to do everything right. This means you must pay close attention to detail. As an American executive expressed it, "The Japanese are fanatics about details. This is why it's exhausting to do business in Japan."

FOR LARGE COMPANIES

1. *Select and train your best people for Japan,* people with technical competence and proven track records. Choose them early if you expect them to become fluent in the language. Leave them in Japan long enough to learn to be effective in dealing with the Japanese. One management consultant told us:

> "The worst thing you can do is send top people for only two or three years. They all want to reorganize and change things. The result is their Japanese managers 'burn out' trying to educate them. After two or three such changes, the Japanese managers just give up."

a. Selection: Choose individuals who have patience, flexibility, sensitivity, integrity, consistency, curiosity and willingness to learn, ability to handle many different kinds of personalities, emotional stability, broad general background, and good health. As mentioned earlier, experience in a foreign country is a great asset, particularly if the person has mastered a foreign language and has lived at least two years overseas.

Families are very important. One of every three cases of business failure is due to family problems for Americans adjusting to Japan. It takes a wife who is very independent and can manage without much help from

her husband, who will not have much time at hor.
Also, no one with serious health problems shou
come. It makes sense to screen the entire family, using a
qualified professional to do the evaluations.

It *is* possible for wives to find jobs in Japan. A placement service offered by Oak Associates in Tokyo has
successfully placed American women in both Japanese
and international firms.

b. Training. Language and cultural background
training should be mandatory for all employees and
their spouses for a minimum of six weeks before leaving
the United States. Language means *total immersion*
(which requires release time from the job). Although
this short training results in achieving only a few polite
phrases, it is still a great help to newcomers. Language
training should continue in Japan with private lessons
several times a week for at least five years if even minimal working skill is expected.

> "We're not sending our best people abroad. The
> Japanese do a much better job of selecting and
> training their people for U.S. assignments. They are
> better educated, better trained, and more compe-
> tent."
>
> President, Japanese subsidiary, American company

> "One of the real difficulties in selecting the best
> employees for an assignment in Japan is the reluc-
> tance of many employees to accept this assign-
> ment. What will happen to him when he returns to
> the American company? Are his talents and experi-
> ence going to be used or will he be sidelined for
> having lost his place on the 'up escalator'?"
>
> American managing director, Tokyo

◄ ◄► ►

2. *When starting a new company in Japan,* set it up as a separate division in the company with direct access to the CEO at headquarters for at least two or three years. The Japanese company must receive adequate financial backing. It's important to "fly the flag" for many years before your presence is accepted. "If you don't plan to stick it out for ten years in Japan, don't bother"—we heard this or something similar from almost every executive interviewed. After the Japanese company is well established, it can be integrated into the structure of the U.S. company.

3. *Register your trademark and patents immediately.* Before you print any letterhead or promotional flyers, ask your attorney in Japan to register your trademarks and patents. Otherwise, you may lose them. It has happened.

4. *Don't be afraid of the Japanese market.* First, investigate the market thoroughly. Spend as much time as needed to develop the right contacts and find the best personnel. Build your reputation slowly for the long term. High-quality products with proper service will do well, but remember, your Japanese connections are vital at every stage.

5. *Japan is unique.* It is *not* a good idea to use Japan as your headquarters for a Far Eastern operation. Japan is totally different from other Far Eastern cultures such as China, Korea, and Malaysia. Also, we were told that, for a variety of reasons, it is not a good idea to choose a manager from Hong Kong or Southeast Asia for your Japanese office. Sometimes people from Southeast Asia have acquired a "colonial" mentality, which will be immediately perceived and resented by the Japanese. In

other cases they may have an attitude unsympathetic to Japanese. Also, Japanese are often prejudiced against Southeast Asians.

6. *Do NOT try to run everything from U.S. headquarters.* It is impossible to understand the problems in countries like Japan unless you've worked there. Officers at headquarters tend to be preoccupied with immediate problems in their own office and they often cannot understand what has to be done in foreign countries. In the words of one general manager of an international chemical company:

> "Most U.S. companies that are international still have a basic strategy that is oriented toward the American market. They are simply not interested in foreign markets."

Unfortunately, his assessment is all too accurate.

FOR SMALL BUSINESS
1. *Research the market* carefully before you decide to enter.
2. *Start small.*
3. *Consider finding a Japanese partner.* This is a tactic that can simplify your problems, provided you find the right partner. Your banking contacts can help you. We interviewed several Americans who had done this and were pleased with the results.

Small companies are handicapped because there are no American-based trading companies to handle the shipping of American products to Japan. (There's a hole in the U.S. market for some enterprising company.)

AFTERWORD

友 As mentioned earlier, we spent many months interviewing German business executives for our earlier books for Germans interacting with Americans, French, and Japanese. What struck us most forcefully at the end of the German interviews was the difference in the attitude of German executives in Japan compared to those in Germany.

It was our feeling that the experience of doing business in Japan had energized the Germans. Germans in Japan were much more positive and optimistic in their attitude than were those in Germany. German business has been very successful in Japan, and the challenge of competing with the Japanese seems to have brought out the best business skills in the Germans.

In a similar vein, we believe that the competition of Japanese products has improved the quality and performance of American goods, a change that is beneficial for the whole country. Americans who are old enough to remember the great depression, or fortunate enough to have known grandparents and great-grandparents, know that there was a time when life in the United States was not easy, when people worked very hard and did their best, and when there was pride in craftsmanship and service. Japan reminds us that such high standards still exist, and that, if America is to prosper, it must relearn some old lessons.

The short-term view of American business that focuses on

immediate profits at the expense of research and development is another serious handicap, and to be successful American companies must devise strategies for overcoming this shortsightedness.

Today the price American business pays for its short-term time orientation is nowhere more apparent than in its lack of training of American employees assigned to Japan. In our interviews with American and Japanese executives, we were struck by the great difference in the training the Americans had received compared to that given the Japanese. This difference is due in part to the differences in job mobility: most Japanese interviewees had spent their entire working lives in one company and the companies had long-term plans for their development and training, whereas most American companies are reluctant to spend time and money training an employee who may very well leave to take another job.

A major Japanese company may spend at least fifty thousand dollars training executives to work in the United States. Having recruited a top graduate of one of the best schools (who, incidentally, will have studied English since early childhood), it will assign the employee to work in different divisions of the company before sending him to the United States for an MBA degree. After this advanced training the employee is reassigned to Japan for at least five years, and then is finally assigned to the United States, where he will be given at least five years to prove himself. This system is quite common, and it is estimated that there are ten thousand Japanese in the United States today who have had such extensive training in American business practices and in the English language. We refer our readers to John L. Graham's excellent article (see Reading List) for further details on how Japanese and American companies differ in personnel training.

Recent changes in Japan's economic status reflect the collapse of the steel and ship-building industries and have resulted in sagging revenues for Japanese buisness. These changes, added to the increased competition from other Asian countries, have shaken Japanese business. It is therefore likely that Japanese business will continue to promote hard work and high-quality products while concentrating on diversification in long-term planning.

◄◄►►

This is a short book by design. Most executives are drowning in paper and even those who want to read have little time. We suggest reading this book once, paying particular attention to the organizing frames of culture that provide the context for your own experiences with the Japanese. Then, reread the book and begin to build on those experiences. This method has proved valuable for a German executive, who said about our book on Japan for German business people, "I tell everyone, 'Read this book, then reread it until you really understand how much there is to learn.'"

GLOSSARY

Action chain   An "action chain," a term borrowed from ethology, is a fixed sequence of events in which people alternately release appropriate responses in each other in order to achieve an agreed-upon or predictable goal. The steps or links in the chain are culturally determined and vary from culture to culture. Examples of action chains include courtship, getting married, completing a sale, *nemawashi,* conducting complex political negotiations, and setting up a business.

Amae   *Amae* comes from the verb *amaeru,* which means "to look to others for support and affection." *Amae* is the feeling of nurturing concern for and dependence on another. This is a complex relationship with roots in the deep physical and emotional attachment of children to their mothers. This relationship is later transferred to the child's teachers and ultimately to his boss and others in positions of authority. In business it takes the form of a mentor-protégé relationship. It is not simply one person's dependence on another; there is reciprocity in the relationship. The superior has both an obligation to his protégé and a dependency on him, which arises from the superior's need to be needed. (See Takeo Doi's *The Anatomy of Dependence.)*

Culture   "Culture" is a technical term used by anthropologists to refer to a system for creating, sending, storing, and processing information evolved by human beings and differentiating them from other life forms. The terms "mores," "tradition," "custom," "habit," and others are subsumed under the cultural umbrella.

Sometimes "culture" is used to refer to art and literature. While art and literature indeed form an important part of culture, we use the term in its wider context in this book.

Congruence   Congruence refers to such matters as appropriateness, how well things work, and the degree to which they fit together. This applies not only to words, but also to behavior and setting. A master of the Tea Ceremony is a master, in part, because of his great sensitivity to congruence.

Haragei   Literally, stomach. Nonverbal form of communication by which one "senses" what is not said or responds in a subtle, indirect manner. It has been said that *"haragei* is all things to all people." (See Michihiro Matsumoto's *Haragei.)*

High Context and Low Context   Context refers to the fact that when people communicate they take for granted how much the listener knows about the subject under discussion. In low-context communication, the listener knows very little and so must be told practically everything. In high-context communication, the listener is already "contexted," and so does not need to be told very much. For example, twins who have shared a long life in proximity to one another work at a much higher level on the context scale than people of different cultures who have only just met.

Informatics   Informatics is a term suggested by MIT mathematician-philosopher Gian-Carlo Rota as a way of identifying the information component (on all levels) of any given extension of the human organism. Informatics refers to the meaning attached to culture-based systems, ranging from toolmaking, technology, language, art, and architecture to social status and behavior.

Interfacing   The term "interfacing" derives from the technical terminology of computers. Computers are modeled after the human brain and have some similarities to cultures in the way they are organized and work. Creating the proper interface is nothing more than creating a system for translating the messages of one part of the computer or a program to another, and it is the key to combining and using different systems. Overcoming the difficulties inherent in interfacing between such contradictory systems as monochronic and polychronic time, for example, requires conscious effort and much goodwill before things begin to work as expected.

Monochronic and Polychronic   Monochronic cultures or situations stress a high degree of scheduling, one thing at a time (hence the name), and an elaborate code of behavior built around promptness in meeting obligations and appointments.

Polychronic cultures are just the opposite. Human relationships are valued over arbitrary schedules and appointments. Many things may happen at once, since many people are involved in everything, and interruptions are frequent.

Nemawashi   A term that means literally "root-binding" or laying the groundwork. This refers to a technique of transplanting trees. Before a tree can be transplanted it is dug out and some roots are cut. Straw and rope are then wrapped around these roots and the tree is put back in the same place for a year or longer to see if it survives. If it does, the tree is then transplanted to another site.

The Japanese use *nemawashi* in virtually everything they do. They always prepare carefully for the next step and avoid any precipitous action. They make sure there will be no unexpected obstacles in their path by laying the groundwork properly. *Nemawashi* takes time, and, because it is crucial to success, one must learn to do the *nemawashi* for everything in Japan. Any effort to shortcut this process is doomed to failure.

Proxemics   A term that refers to man's use of space as an aspect of his culture; conversational distance, design of interior spaces, the layout of a town, etc. See Edward T. Hall's book *The Hidden Dimension*.

Reference Group   The term refers to those people who are significant in a person's life. The reference group can be in business or in social life. It can also include neighbors whose opinions are important. It is the feedback from this group that is used by an individual to determine whether or not his behavior and performance are satisfactory.

Screen-dependent and screen-independent These terms refer to people's needs for sensory screening in situations where they must concentrate or which are defined as "private." In Germany, the screens take the form of soundproof walls and doors. This is because Germans are very sensitive to auditory intrusions and are more distracted by noise than the Japanese or such Mediterranean peoples as the Greeks and Italians. The Germans and Northern Europeans are largely screen-dependent. The Japanese are just the opposite.

Situation and Situational Dialects The term situation, as it is used in this book, has a special meaning. Situations are framed and complete in themselves. Thus, a conference, a meal, a visit, buying tickets, writing a letter, courtship, sleeping, getting dressed, greeting, reading a book, and studying are all situations.

One of the most efficient ways to learn a language is to learn the languages of different situations. These are called "situational dialects."

Zaibatsu Groups of companies representing important industrial sectors of the Japanese economy prior to the end of World War II. The *zaibatsu* consisted of twenty to thirty major firms clustered around a large bank. Each company had its satellite supply companies. A typical *zaibatsu* might include a steel company, trading company, automobile company, insurance company, etc. *Zaibatsus* had enormous power and influence. Although they were officially disbanded after the war, their influence networks remain.

READING LIST

Books published in Japan are available in Western hotel bookstores and at major bookstores in Tokyo. In the United States, many major cities have bookstores specializing in Japanese books, such as Kodansha International with its branches in New York, Los Angeles, and San Francisco.

◄ ◄►►

Abegglen, James C., and Stalk, George, Jr. *Kaisha, the Japanese Corporation.* New York: Basic Books, 1985.

Alden, Vernon R. "The Trade Deficit: Stop Looking for Scapegoats." *Business Week,* April 8, 1985.

American Chamber of Commerce in Japan "High Adventure in Joint Ventures—Revisited." Tokyo, 1972.

Benedict, Ruth *The Chrysanthemum and the Sword.* Tokyo: Charles E. Tuttle, 1946; Boston: Houghton Mifflin; New York: New American Library.

Browning, E. S. "Tough Nut to Crack." *The Wall Street Journal,* May 20, 1985.

Chira, Susan "A Tough Ascent for Japanese Woman." New York *Times,* February 24, 1985.

——"Reader's Digest Leaves Japan." New York *Times,* December 25, 1985.

Christopher, Robert C. *The Japanese Mind: The Goliath Explained.* New York: Linden Press/Simon & Schuster, 1983.

————*Second to None: American Companies in Japan.* New York: Crown, 1986.

Deutsch, Mitchell F. *Doing Business with the Japanese.* New York: New American Library, 1984.

Doi, Takeo *The Anatomy of Dependence.* New York: Kodansha International/Harper & Row, 1976.

Drucker, Peter F. "American-Japanese Realities." *The Wall Street Journal,* October 11, 1985.

————"Japan and Adversarial Trade." *The Wall Street Journal,* April 1, 1986.

————*Management Tasks, Responsibilities, Practices.* New York: Harper & Row, 1974.

————*Managing in Turbulent Times.* New York: Harper & Row, 1980.

————"Playing in the Information-Based Orchestra." *The Wall Street Journal,* June 4, 1985.

Field, George *From Bonsai to Levi's: When West Meets East: An Insider's Surprising Account of How the Japanese Live.* New York: Macmillan, 1983.

Fujiwara, Mariko *Hitonami: Keeping Up with the Satos.* Tokyo: Hakuhodo Institute of Life and Living, 1983.

————*Japanese Women in Turmoil.* Tokyo: Hakuhodo Institute of Life and Living, 1984.

Garfinkel, Perry "The Best Jewish Mother in the World." *Psychology Today,* September, 1983.

Gibney, Frank *Japan: The Fragile Super Power.* New York: New American Library, 1980.

————*Miracle by Design: The Real Reasons Behind Japan's Economic Success.* New York: Times Books, 1982.

Goffman, Erving *The Presentation of Self in Everyday Life.* Garden City, N.Y.: Doubleday, 1983.

Graham, John L., and Sano, Yoshihiro *Smart Bargaining: Doing Business with the Japanese*. Cambridge, Mass.: Ballinger, 1984.

Graham, John L. "Today the Summit—Tomorrow, Business." New York *Times*, May 5, 1986.

Hadamitzki, Wolfgang, and Spahn, Mark *Kanji and Kana*. Tokyo: Charles E. Tuttle, 1981.

Halberstam, David *The Reckoning*. New York: William Morrow, 1986.

Hall, Edward T. *The Silent Language* New York: Anchor Books/Doubleday, 1959.

——*The Hidden Dimension*. New York: Anchor Books/Doubleday, 1966.

——*Beyond Culture*. New York: Anchor Books/Doubleday, 1976.

——*The Dance of Life: The Other Dimension of Time*. New York: Anchor Books/Doubleday, 1983.

(All of Hall's books are available in Japanese.)

Imai, Masaaki *16 Ways to Avoid Saying No*. Tokyo: Nihon Keizai Shimbun, 1981.

——*Never Take Yes for an Answer*. Tokyo: Simul Press, 1975.

Irish, Jeffrey S. "A Yank Learns to Bow." New York *Times Sunday Magazine*, June 8, 1986.

Japan Airlines *A Businessman's Guide to Japan*. 1982.

Japan Institute for Social and Economic Affairs *Japan 1985, An International Comparison*. Tokyo: Keizai Koho Center, 1984. (Facts and figures on everything from advertising to working hours. Invaluable reference handbook.)

JETRO (Japan External Trade Organization) *Doing Business in Japan*. Tokyo: Gakuseisha Publishing Co., 1984.

Johnson, Chalmers *MITI and the Japanese Miracle: The Growth of Industrial Policy, 1925–75*. Stanford, Cal.: Stanford University Press, 1982.

Kinji Kawamura Foreign Press Center *Japan, A Pocket Guide*. Tokyo, 1984. (Excellent summaries on media, education, labor, etc.)

Kobayashi, Kauro "How to Win a Negotiation—Japanese Style." *News from Hotel Okura*, August, 1984, vol. 8, no. 8. Available upon request to Planning & Promotion Division, Hotel Okura. Reprinted from *Japan Economic Journal*, July 31, 1984.

Lachia, Eduardo "Exemplary Envoy." *The Wall Street Journal*, January 2, 1985.

Lebra, Takie Sugiyama *Japanese Women: Constraint and Fulfillment*. Honolulu: University of Hawaii Press, 1984.

———*Japanese Patterns of Behavior*. Honolulu: University of Hawaii Press, 1976.

Maloney, Don "East Is East—Or Is It?" in *Speaking of Japan (The Forum for Corporate Communications)*. Tokyo: Keizai Koho Center, June 1982.

Martin, Bradley K. "Japan's Trading Giants Look to the Year 2000." *The Wall Street Journal*, March 31, 1986.

Matsumoto, Michihiro *Haragei*. Tokyo: Kodansha Ltd., 1984.

Miller, Roy Andrew *Japan's Modern Myth, The Language and Beyond*. New York and Tokyo: John Weatherhill, 1982.

Morley, John David *Pictures from the Water Trade: Adventures of a Westerner in Japan*. New York: Atlantic Monthly Press, 1985.

Nakane, Chie *Japanese Society*. Berkeley: University of California Press, 1970.

Norbury, Paul, and Bownas, Geoffrey *Business in Japan*. Inverness: Macmillan Press Ltd. and Paul Norbury Press Ltd., 1980.

Ohmae, Kenichi *Triad Power: The Coming Shape of Global Competition*. New York: Free Press, 1985.

Ouchi, William *The M-Form Society: How American Team-work Can Recapture the Competitive Edge*. Reading, Mass.: Addison-Wesley, 1985.

——*Theory Z*. New York: Avon Books, 1980.

Pascale, Richard T., and Athos, Anthony G. *The Art of Japanese Management*. New York: Simon & Schuster, 1981.

Passin, Herbert *Japanese and the Japanese: Language and Culture Change*. Tokyo: Kinseido Ltd., 1980.

Peters, Thomas J., and Waterman, Robert H., Jr. *In Search of Excellence: Lessons from America's Best-Run Companies*. New York: Warner Books, 1984.

Reischauer, Edwin *The Japanese*. Cambridge, Mass.: Harvard University Press, 1978.

Rohlen, Thomas *For Harmony and Strength*. Berkeley: University of California Press, 1974.

Rosecrance, Richard *The Rise of the Trading State*. New York: Basic Books, 1985.

Rudofsky, Bernard *The Kimono Mind*. Garden City, N.Y.: Doubleday, 1965.

Smith, Robert J. *Japanese Society: Tradition, Self, and the Social Order*. Cambridge: Cambridge University Press, 1983.

Sogo, Shinsaku "Gaining Respect: The ABCs of How to Get Along With Your Japanese Staff." *Speaking of Japan*. Tokyo: Keizai Koho Center, March 1981.

Stevenson, Harold W., Lee, Shin-ying, and Stigler, James W. "Mathematics Achievement of Chinese, Japanese, and American Children." *Science*, February 14, 1986.

Storry, Richard *A History of Modern Japan*. New York: Penguin Books, 1982.

Taylor, Jared *Shadows of the Rising Sun*. New York: William Morrow, 1983.

Thurow, Lester C. *The Zero-Sum Solution*. New York: Simon & Schuster, 1985.

Time Special Issue on Japan, August 1, 1983.

——"Swamped by Japan." April 15, 1985.

Tung, Rosalie L. *Business Negotiations with the Japanese*. Lexington, Mass.: D. C. Heath, 1984.

Van Zandt, Howard F. *New Facts About Japanese and Americans*. Tokyo: Charles E. Tuttle, 1971.

Varley, Paul H. *Japanese Culture: A Short History*. New York: Charles E. Tuttle, 1974.

Vogel, Ezra F. *Japan As Number 1: Lessons for America*. New York: Harper & Row, 1980.

Wagatsuma, Hiroshi, and Rosett, Arthur "Cultural Attitudes Towards Contract Law: Japan and the United States Compared." *Pacific Basin Law Journal,* 2:76, 1983.

Wagatsuma, Hiroshi, and De Vos, George A. *Heritage of Endurance: Family Patterns and Delinquency Formation in Urban Japan*. Berkeley: University of California Press, 1983.

Wall Street Journal "Working Like a Log." April 6, 1984.

Wysocki, Bernard "Lust for Labor." *The Wall Street Journal,* April 21, 1986.

Zimmerman, Mark *How to Do Business with the Japanese: A Strategy for Success*. New York: Random House, 1985.

INDEX

Action chains, 30–32; defined, 157

Advertising, 31, 102, 116, 138–41

Agendas, 19, 21; flexibility and, 114–16; meetings and, 116–17

Aisatsu (greeting ceremony), 118

Amae, 54–56, 68; defined, 157

American business in Japan, 97–129, 131–34; 135–51; advice for, 145–51; checklist for starting, 102–3; collaboration with and use of Japanese employees, 74, 147–48; communication and negotiating and, 114–29, 131, 147; connections and, 103–5, 110–12; entertainment and gifts and, 108–10, 131; executives for, 100–1; saving face and, 124–28; friendships and, 107–8; government's relation to, 91, 92, 133; home office problems, 132–34; initial program for, 99–101; joint ventures, 104; language and, 105–7, 111–12, 118, 146, 149; long-term planning and, 98–103, 146; managing, 131–34; marketing, selling, and distributing, 135–45, 150; meetings and, 116–17; and personnel recruitment, 110–12, 131–34, 148–49, 150; and public relations, 141–43; and quality control, 72, 155; small companies, 151; trade with Japan and, 93–94; and training of personnel, 148, 149, 154. See also Americans

American Chamber of Commerce, 100, 102, 136

Americans (American culture): action chains and, 30–32; communication and, 3–4 (see also Communication); contexting and, 8–11, 34–35; and education, 49–50; and information flow, 28–30 (see also Information); and interfacing, 33–35; and Japanese culture compared, 39–53, 79 (see also Japanese; specific aspects); and leadership, 79; and lead time and schedules, 24–25; present- and short-term orientation and, 22; resistance to change, 39; space and, 13, 14, 15 (see also Space); and time orientation (see Time). See also American business in Japan

Appointments, 23, 24–25; and keeping people waiting, 26–27; M-time and P-time and, 17, 18, 19

Attorneys, use of, 128–29

Auditory space and screening, 13–14, 49, 160

Automobiles (cars), 136, 138, 143